Faultless to a Fault

Gaṅgeśa on Upamāna

Faultless to a Fault
Gaṅgeśa on Upamāna
in Indian Epistemology

Uma Chattopadhyay

DK PRINTWORLD
Publishers of Indian Traditions

Cataloging in Publication Data — DK
[Courtesy: D.K. Agencies (P) Ltd. <docinfo@dkagencies.com>]

Chattopadhyay, Uma, 1955- **author.**
Faultless to a fault : Gaṅgeśa on Upamāna in Indian epistemology / Uma Chattopadhyay.
pages cm
Includes bibliographical references (pages).
ISBN 13: 9788124608173

1. Gaṅgeśa, active 13th century. Upamānakhaṇḍa. 2. Upamāna – Early works to 1800. 3. Nyaya – Early works to 1800. I. Title.

DDC 121 23

ISBN 13: 978-81-246-0817-3
First published in India, 2015

Printed and published by:
D.K. Printworld (P) Ltd.
Regd. Office: *Vedaśrī*, F-395, Sudarshan Park
(Metro Station: Ramesh Nagar), New Delhi – 110 015
Phones: (011) 2545 3975, 2546 6019; *Fax*: (011) 2546 5926
e-mail: indology@dkprintworld.com
Website: www.dkprintworld.com

In

Memory of those who are now
all lighting stars of my life

Srikrishna Chattopadhyay (father)
Pannalal Bandyopadhyay (father-in-law)
Gita Chattopadhyay (mother)
Anima Bandyopadhyay (mother-in-law)

Preface

It is by the *ahaitukī kṛpā* of my mother Ananandamayee that I could complete the book, *Faultless to a Fault: Gaṅgeśa on Upamāna in Indian Epistemology*. I had to cross many hurdles including the sudden demise of my elder and only sister Gouri Mukherjee very recently on 17 May 2014. I cannot think about my family, past and present, without my dearest *dīdī*. There was a great vacuum in my life. With a heavy heart, I had to come back to the work of finishing this book. I had been deeply involved in the study and understanding of Indian philosophy from the early stages of my academic career and had a rare opportunity to study many branches of it including the Nyāya system from stalwarts like Prof. Pradyot Kumar Mukhopadhyay, Prof. Kali Krishna Banerjee, Prof. Srilekha Dutta, Prof. Krishna Roy, Pandit Pañcānan Śāstrī, Pandit Narmada Tarkatīrtha, Prof. Tapan Kumar Chakraborty, Prof. Sukhoranjan Saha and many other eminent teachers of the philosophy world. How much knowledge I acquired from them I do not know; at least what I gained from them is to love Indian philosophy and culture of this nation. And my commitment to this tradition came from them, I believe.

The ability of Indian philosophers to understand the depth of a problem and their potential to resolve the same are amazing to me. What I learned from my teachers was to address a problem applying both Indian and Western philosophies. It is a rare kind of inspiration that I got from the academia of Jadavpur University's philosophy department. I have to acknowledge the contribution from an illustrious teacher Prof. Pranab Kumar Sen. He always inspired us by saying "You have to play in the field, going beyond merely watching and making comments on others". This was really a valuable advice for me. Guided by such stimulated advices and due to my deep love for studies in the Nyāya tradition, I started the work on Gaṅgeśa's *Upamānacintāmaṇi*, a part of his monumental work *Tattvacintāmaṇi*, though knowing fully that I was not competent enough to understand thoroughly a Navya-Nyāya philosopher like Gaṅgeśa Upādhyāya. Then why and how did I come to understand Gaṅgeśa?

In my undergraduate course, I was surprised to notice a problem regarding *upamāna pramāṇa* (knowledge by comparison) besides many other problems of Indian and Western philosophies. While studying Udayanācārya's *Nyāyakusumānjaliḥ* in my post-graduate course, I was surprised to see that both the Nyāya and Mīmāṁsā systems are accepting this source of knowledge but totally in two different senses. After completing my Master's, I got the rare opportunity of doing Ph.D. under the guidance of Prof. Pradyot Kumar Mukhopadhyay. I changed my initial research topic on Indian scepticism (*apramā*) and took finally *upamāna* as topic for my research. I immediately realized that under his able guidance I will be able to swim (at least to some extent) in the ocean of philosophy. It took a long time, but I could complete my research in the mid-1990s. The subject was vast as I considered all the schools of Indian tradition in the context of *upamāna*. I developed the first part of my work and later made it a publication *Dishonoured by Philosophers: Upamāna in Indian Epistemology* where I have discussed the debates between Nyāya–Bauddha, Nyāya–Vaiśeṣika and also Nyāya–Mīmāṁsā, etc.

Historically I have made a story on *upamāna* from Gautama to Udayanācārya (the story from the fifth to the eleventh century CE) regarding the issue of *upamāna*. Of course, the development is mainly logical, but to some extent historical. I ended the research dissertation with the view of Gaṅgeśa on *upamāna*. It is really a brilliant feature that most of the philosophers including some Nyāya–Vaiśeṣikas have either shown indifference or raised objections and showed that Nyāya position is faulty but all the three stalwart philosophers of the Nyāya tradition ranging from the fifth to the twelfth century – Gautama, Udayanācārya and Gaṅgeśa – are given much importance to the problem of *upamāna*. Final faultless position is shown by Gaṅgeśa. Gautama and Udayanācārya are comparatively lighter than Gaṅgeśa. I had to complete the story of *upamāna* (with the help of my teacher and with my very limited capacity) by Gaṅgeśa.

In my previous book I could not include Gaṅgeśa's view on *upamāna* but I thought that if possible I might prepare another dissertation on *upamāna* where Gaṅgeśa would be focused. The text *Upamānacintāmaṇi* is very hard and full of Navya-Nyāya technicalities; so I have tried to present Gaṅgeśa not by literal translation but only the idea of Gaṅgeśa in today's language. This is to complete a story and to show how much the philosophers of Indian soil are committed to their own tradition, which is full of rationality. So presentation of Gaṅgeśa is not only the outcome of my emotions but is academically argued. This is actually a continuation of the first book. I have only tried to make a gateway to the future researchers on Indian philosophy. I have presented Gaṅgeśa in two chapters. But before that and before giving Gaṅgeśa's final answer, one external objection is raised in the first chapter, i.e. insertion of *upamāna* makes the scheme of *pramāṇa*s anomalous. It would have been better if Gautama or Gaṅgeśa could delete *upamāna* from their scheme of *pramāṇa*s. I have given an alternative answer and finally a positive answer in favour of the Nyāya position.

I am happy that I could complete this book after five years of publishing of my first book. I am late as I was heavily engaged in my departmental activities. As an acting coordinator I had to take responsibilities of many publications and UGC-SAP-DRS programmes, and my personal academic programme of publication was postponed. My desire was immense but possibility of giving shape to it was disturbed. I had to accept the delay.

The fact that I could complete the present work was made possible by the direct and indirect contributions of many. The foremost among them is my husband Arun Bandyopadhyay, who currently holds Nurul Hasan Chair Professor of History at the University of Calcutta. He first suggested the idea of completing this book on Gaṅgeśa as a search for perfection in our arguments for *upamāna* – faultless to a fault. But his constant pestering for finishing the book was creating a kind of nervousness in me. It is only because of him that I could prepare this book. He is always positive for my academic pursuits. I always believe if research is one step, publishing it is another step. I was reluctant to take the second step; it is only for Arun that I have crossed the second step and the idea of Gaṅgeśa in the present form could see the light of the day.

This time I am deeply indebted to my very dear daughter-in-law Amrita (Manorama) and my son Manasij (Bapan). Their peaceful, enjoyable and creative life is a real inspiration for me. I can do many positive things when they are happy. My daughter-in-law even went further and used to ask me the question whether her telephone call from England was creating disturbance to my studies. A computer engineer by profession, she has always appeared beautiful and nice to me. Her finer senses are really attractive and much inspiring. May God bless them for their health and good soul. Her father Shri Gautam Bhattacharya (Bhaiti), mother Smt. Bhaswati Bhattacharya (Deepsikha) and younger sister Arpita (Mimburi) are my constant inspiration in academic journey. I am really grateful to them. I am immensely indebted to them in many ways. May God bless us for this beautiful bonding.

The five other young stars – Bishnupriya (a very good classical vocalist), Nandini, Anindita, Somapriya and Ayanika – have always worked as sources of inspiration. And they are full of qualities and stand always by my side in different ways. They know how much valuable is their inspiration for me and in which way they can all help me. I am also happy with the kids of my family. They are my inspiration. They are Baby Queen, Ganubhai, Gunudidi, Gopal and Gadadhar. My two sister-in-laws, Didibhai (Amita Chakraborty) and Baby (Anindita Chatterjee), are always with me. I could make myself more creative by their sweet presence in my life. My another extended sister Mitra, despite our infrequent meetings in recent times, silently make a positive presence in my life. I do always cherish her company.

By the help and support from the domestic ladies – Roma, Anita and Seema – I could take much time from the regular household works.

My indebtedness to Mrs Tapati Mitra is immense. Her meticulous typing with the diacritical mark is really praiseworthy. I pray blessings of my mother for her and for her beautiful family.

I cannot thank my teacher, Prof. Pradyot Kumar Mukhopadhyay; so I take this opportunity to convey my *praṇāma* to him. I beg his blessings which will help me in every way.

I am immensely grateful to our Hon'ble Vice-Chancellor Prof. Suranjan Das. His academic inspiration is unforgettable. I feel proud when I see a dynamic personality like Prof. Das is leading the University of Calcutta for its academic excellence.

Some of the portions of the present work I presented in refresher courses, orientation programmes, and seminars in different universities and colleges and the feedback that I received is really unforgettable. That made me to think and re-think on different issues particularly on the issue of similarity, place of *upamāna* in the scheme and also regarding the independent status of *upamāna* in the scheme of *pramāṇa*. My thanks to all such participants of refresher courses and orientation programmes. We not only teach in the courses, we learn immensely from them. So I am obliged to the participants, to the directors of academic staff colleges, and the coordinators of such programmes and the organizers of different seminars.

I am very happy with the production of my previous book by Shri Susheel Mittal of D.K. Printworld (Delhi). So this time also I wanted him to take up the responsibility. D.K. Printworld's ethics and production method are really amazing. Distance is not at all a factor for a good job. This is proved by the dedication of Shri Susheel Mittal and his company D.K. Printworld. I am happy and deeply obliged to him.

I cannot convey my thanks to my Ph.D. scholars, but I can convey my blessings for their academic support which they have given in their own way. I need to mention specially the name of Mr Siddique Alam Beg, my Ph.D. scholar. He was all the time ready to bring books from different corners. May God bless him for his academic enthusiasm.

My close neighbours Krishna and Kanchan are always with me and have very much inspired me for my academic and professional activities. I am grateful to them for their positive role.

There are many colleagues in my department and in the other departments with whom I made my academic communications that enriched myself. Of them, special mention can be made of Dr Sharmistha Bakshi, Dr Krishna Chatterjee, Prof. Subirranjan Bhattacharya, Prof. Manidipa Sanyal, Prof. Nini Chanda, Prof. Aparna Banerjee, Prof. Priyambada Sarkar, Prof. Dilip Kumar Mohanta, Dr Shilpita Mitra, Dr Shyamasree Bhattacharya, Dr Mahjabeen Jahan, Dr Pralayankar Bhattacharyya and Smt. Sunanda Das and many others. I must also mention the names of Prof. Indrani Sanyal of the Department of Philosophy, Jadavpur University, and Prof. Amarnath Bhattacharya, retired professor of philosophy, Burdwan University who have always enlightened me by their brilliant observations, communications and conversations. I always enjoy teaching, so the past and the present students influence me in my thought process. I convey my blessings to them all.

Kolkata **Uma Chattopadhyay**
23 October 2014

Contents

1

Setting the Theme
Upamāna's Journey from Many Faults to the Faultless

I

AT the outset I must mention that this book is a sequel to my previous book entitled *Dishonoured by Philosophers: Upamāna in Indian Epistemology* (2009). In the first book, I introduced the notion of *upamāna*, its definition, process and also its status in Indian epistemology in general and the Nyāya school in particular. The book ends with the view of Udayanācārya, an eleventh-century philosopher. According to this view (of course, according to all Naiyāyikas), *upamāna* is an irreducible independent *pramāṇa*-like perception, inference and testimony, and the *pramāṇa* is important in a special context of knowledge relating to word–meaning relation. The process of knowledge is as follows. When one does not know what exactly is the animal "bison", one has only a testimonial knowledge of the form that a bison is like a cow from a reliable person. The person in another place such as forest or zoo garden perceives an animal which has similarity with a cow – there the person not only perceives the similarity of a cow in the present animal, but in addition to that he remembers the meaning of the previously heard sentence (*atideśa vākyārtha*) that a bison is like a cow. Then on the basis of all the previous conditions he knows something new. He comes to know that the animal which is present before him must be the same as the meaning of the word "bison". And he generally understands that "this is a bison":

Prasiddhasādharmyātsādhyasādhanam upamānam |
– *Nyāya-sūtra* 1.1.1

An interesting feature of Nyāya philosophy is that among the four *pramāṇa*s (sources of valid cognition), all the above-mentioned *pramāṇa*s are *vastugrāhaka*s (methods or sources for knowing the object) while *upamāna* is the only *pramāṇa* which is *śaktigrāhaka* (method or source for knowing the word–object relation). One interesting feature in the area of Nyāya language philosophy is this. The Naiyāyikas admit eight kinds of *śaktigrāhaka*s (method for knowing word meaning) for the knowledge of word–meaning relation. Among these eight kinds of *grāhaka*s, all the seven *grāhaka*s are ultimately reducible to any of the seven *pramāṇa*s like perception. Among the eight, only *upamāna* is irreducible to the other *pramāṇa*s. It is irreducible and it has a very definite status.

Many of the Indian philosophers have taken the hard task of reducing *upamāna* to other *pramāṇa*s, but all such reductions are fallacious (Uma Chattopadhyay 2009). The Vaiśeṣikas of the sister system of Nyāya school have taken the task of reducing *upamāna* to *anumāna* but that is ultimately logically unacceptable. I have shown all such reductions in my previous book. Different alternative objections are raised against the Nyāya theory of *upamāna*. The Buddhists, the Vaiśeṣikas and even a so-called Nyāya philosopher Bhāsarvajña (Nyāyaikadeśī) also raised strong objections against such a *pramāṇa* which is important for the knowledge of word–meaning relation. The interesting feature of the debate is that it draws our attention to the fact that the Buddhists, the Sāṁkhyas, the Jainas or the Cārvākas can raise objection. But why the sister system of Nyāya, the Vaiśeṣika school or Bhāsarvajña who belongs to the Nyāya school itself are not in favour of this *upamāna pramāṇa*? When so many objections are against the admission of *upamāna*, naturally those objections weaken the Nyāya theory of *upamāna*. So the Nyāya theory appears to be a false theory, a weak theory or at least there is great fault in the theory of *upamāna* of the Naiyāyikas – it is better to discard *upamāna* from the scheme of *pramāṇa*s which according to them consists four in number.

In my previous book, the objections of the Bauddhas, Jainas, Sāṁkhyas, Vaiśeṣikas, Cārvāka and also philosopher Bhāsarvajña are shown, and at the same time the answers from the Nyāya viewpoint are given. The answers in relation to Gautama's *upamāna* are given from Vātsyāyana, Jayantabhaṭṭa and finally from Udayanācārya. Jayantabhaṭṭa is generally regarded as belonging to the old Nyāya tradition while Udayanācārya comes between old and Navya-Nyāya tradition. Udayanācārya sometimes is regarded as the founder of Navya-Nyāya tradition as he has combined the Nyāya and Vaiśeṣika together, known as the syncretic school of Nyāya–Vaiśeṣika. After Udayanācārya, in the twelfth century, the stalwart Navya-Naiyāyika Gaṅgeśa Upādhyāya in his monumental work *Tattvacintāmaṇi* gave a definite place to *upamāna*. Accordingly, he wrote *Pratyakṣacintāmaṇi*, *Anumānacintāmaṇi*, *Upamānacintāmaṇi* and *Śabdacintāmaṇi*. When already so many objections were prevailing in the philosophical literature, he could easily discard this debatable *pramāṇa* from the scheme, and he could do a kind of logical economy (*lāghava*) by advocating a scheme of *pramāṇa* by three. Instead of that, he made *upamāna* at par with the other *pramāṇa*s. He again reopened the question of *upamāna* in a dialogical method, which is the beauty of Indian tradition.

After Gaṅgeśa many commentators wrote rich commentaries on Gaṅgeśa's *Tattvacintāmaṇi* but they have ignored *Upamānacintāmaṇi*. As for example, Mathuranatha, while writing commentary on other parts of *Tattvacintāmaṇi*, did not give attention to *Upamānacintamaṇi* and *upamāna*. This fact may remind us to think about the objections raised by the Buddhists or Bhāsarvajña, etc. against *upamāna*. But the very fact that both Gautama, the propounder of *Nyāya-Sūtra*, and Gaṅgeśa have written about all the four *pramāṇa*s. He writes in the *sūtra*

1.1.3: *pratyakṣānumānaupamāna śabdapramāṇāni* (perception, inference, analogy and *śabda* are the four *pramāṇas*). Writing after many years, knowing fully well about the objections, Gaṅgeśa Upādhyāya defended the same scheme of *pramāṇas* of four admitted by Gautama which includes *upamāna*. *Upamāna* is the third independent *pramāṇa*. Among the commentators of *Tattvacintāmaṇi* only Pragalbhācārya, a later commentator, has written a *ṭīkā* known as *Pragalvī* on Gaṅgeśa's *Upamānacintāmaṇi*. Intervention of Gaṅgeśa and his commentator Pragalbhācārya inspires us to rethink and open the dialogue about the faultless *upamāna* which according to many is a false theory, as it is unacceptable or appears as weak or a reducible source of knowledge. This we can see through Gaṅgeśa. So the book will consider the view about *upamāna* from Gaṅgeśa's standpoint. I consider Gaṅgeśa's standpoint a height of perfection, the most vigorous defence in a series of defences and objections, and I call it *Faultless to a Fault*, the main title of my present work.

II

One important point that we need to notice here before going to the text under consideration is this: before going to the problem, we need to look at the problem related to *upamāna* historically. When we study the literature of old Naiyāyikas, we find the opponents are mainly the Bauddhas. In *Ratnakīrtinibandhāvalī*, Ratnakīrti has taken much care in criticizing the Nyāya theory of *upamāna*. He has shown with many other objections that word–meaning relation is false or meaningless. Accordingly, there is no question of knowing the meaning relation and there is no place for *upamāna pramāṇa*. In the eleventh century, Udayanācārya has shown the weakness of the Buddhist position and established the Nyāya theory of *upamāna*. The interesting fact is that the strong opposition came from the Buddhists and not from the Mīmāṁsakas. So in the Nyāya literature we find that most of the objections are raised against the Buddhist position and not against the Mīmāṁsā. But strong objections the Naiyāyikas could raise against the Mīmāṁsakas, as the Mīmāṁsakas, though they admit *upamāna* as an independent *pramāṇa*, admit it in an absolutely different sense. We have already mentioned that the Naiyāyikas admit *upamāna* for the knowledge of meaning relation, the Mīmāṁsakas admit *upamāna* for the knowledge of unperceived similarity from the knowledge of perceived similarity:

> *upamānamapisadr̥śyaṁasannikr̥ṣṭe arthe buddhim utpādayati yathā gavaya darśanaṁ gosmaraṇasya iti* ।
>
> – Śabarasvāmī 1883: 12

According to the Prābhākara Mīmāṁsakas, similarity (*sādr̥śya*) is an independent irreducible *padārtha* (category) and when we know unperceived similarity from perceived similarity we need to admit the process of *upamāna*. Ratnakīrti, the Buddhist philosopher, while criticizing the theory of *upamāna*, did the same against both the Nyāya theory of *upamāna* and Mīmāṁsā theory of *upamāna*. To establish the Nyāya theory of *upamāna*, one needs to make the thesis absolutely different from the Mīmāṁsā theory of *upamāna*. Gaṅgeśa has done the same. In his *Upamānacintāmaṇi*, his main opponents are Mīmāṁsakas, particularly the Prābhākaras, as they admit that *sādr̥śya* is an independent category and for the knowledge of unperceived similarity one needs the *upamāna pramāṇa*. To take an example, a person knows from perception or reliable sentence that a bison is similar to a cow. The person when perceives a bison he knows the similarity of a bison in the unperceived (at that moment) cow which may be existing in his house. He may utter the sentence "my cow has the similarity of this bison". This knowledge cannot be explained by only perception or inference or testimony or not even by *arthāpatti* (postulation) or *anupalabdhi* (non-cognition). This is an independent kind of knowledge, which is *upamiti* and the process is *upamāna*. In *Ratnakīrtinibandhāvalī*, Ratnakīrti has shown that Mīmāṁsā theory of *upamāna* is not acceptable as *sādr̥śya* is a misnomal notion. It is *alīka* or *tuccha* (fictitious). So for the knowledge of *sādṛśya*, there is no need of an independent *pramāṇa upamāna* (Uma Chattopadhyay 2009: 40-41). Later, Udayanācārya has shown that similarity is a real entity. Without the admission of similarity, our experience of sameness is not explainable. Of course, according to him, similarity is an acceptable *padārtha* but is not irreducible independent category. He has also discarded the view that *upamāna* is to be accepted for the knowledge of similarity. *Upamāna*, according to Udayanācārya, is for the knowledge of meaning relation.

III

This is an important feature in the world of Indian philosophy in the twelfth century that the positions of the Buddhist philosophy declined. As a consequence to that, Gaṅgeśa was not facing the Buddhist opposition. But this is not enough to see the Nyāya position. The Mīmāṁsā position was prevalent at that time. The debate between Nyāya and Mīmāṁsā became inevitable. To establish the Nyāya position, Gaṅgeśa had to face the Mīmāṁsā opposition. But the opposition of Mīmāṁsā was very strong and it was really difficult to combat with the Mīmāṁsā view. The position was difficult because from the Mīmāṁsā point, there is no question apparently to discard the *upamāna pramāṇa*. In whole Indian philosophical tradition, only these two schools admit *upamāna*. And both of them admit that the *upamāna pramāṇa* (at least as the source of knowledge) involves the notion of similarity (*sādṛśya*). So both of them have given the name *upamāna* (*upamā* = *sādṛśya*, i.e. comparison means similarity). From this it appears that both the schools are same with regard to *upamāna* (the status, nature, resulting knowledge, etc.). But the understanding of the two systems shows that the Naiyāyikas admit *upamāna* for the knowledge of meaning relation, while the Mīmāṁsakas admit for the knowledge of similarity. Second, Mīmāṁsā *upamāna* as a process involves similarity (*sādṛśya*) and as a result also (*upamiti*) involves similarity while according to the Naiyāyikas *upamāna* as a process involves similarity but as a result is the knowledge of word–meaning relation, and not merely knowledge of similarity. So in a sense the two schools have totally different views regarding *upamāna*. Only as both of them consider similarity in the process, both have given the name of *pramāṇa upamāna* (comparison). Moreover, though both the schools admit similarity, both of them are not in favour of admitting *sādṛśya* (similarity) as an independent irreducible category.

The Mīmāṁsakas have taken the more stronger position than the Naiyāyikas. According to the Mīmāṁsā school (particularly the Prābhākara), similarity is an irreducible *padārtha*, a category and a specific kind of knowledge – for such category similarity the *upamāna pramāṇa* is admitted as an independent *pramāṇa*. This makes us to think that to show finally the Nyāya view faultless the Naiyāyikas are to face the Mīmāṁsā opposition. This opposition of the Mīmāṁsā is stronger than the previous oppositions like the Buddhists or Vaiśeṣikas. Because both the schools are realists and at the same time pluralist, and both of them admit *upamāna*. Why then so difference? Could the Nyāya reduce this knowledge to any other *pramāṇa*? Gaṅgeśa's answer is negative. His consideration of *upamāna* reminds us to think that *upamāna* is to be accepted as an independent *pramāṇa* for the knowledge of a particular variety of meaning relation. Even after the decline of the Buddhists, the Vaiśeṣika, Sāṁkhya and Jaina positions were also shadowed by the Mīmāṁsā position which remained strong. Accordingly, to establish the Nyāya position, the Naiyāyikas need to show the weakness of the Mīmāṁsā position. They now need to show that the Nyāya theory of *upamāna* is faultless by independent reasons. Gaṅgeśa in the twelfth century has done the same in his *Upamānacintāmaṇi*, a part of his monumental work *Tattvacintāmaṇi*. First, he has shown that similarity is a fact and we have some behaviour involving similarity. But the similarity is not an independent irreducible category (*svatantra padārtha*). It can be reduced to some other category. Gaṅgeśa by his dialogical method has reduced it to *sāmānya* (universal). Second, Gaṅgeśa has taken the responsibility to show that *upamāna* in the Nyāya sense is irreducible independent *pramāṇa* and is not at par with the Mīmāṁsā theory. As a result, we find in Gaṅgeśa the faultless position of the *upamāna* thesis. So from Gaṅgeśa's point of view all the other views relating to *upamāna* are faulty, even the position made by Udayana is incomplete as it could not consider the Mīmāṁsā position but Gaṅgeśa's final answer given in *Upamānacintāmaṇi* resolves the *upamāna* debate. So here is the significance of the title of my book on Gaṅgeśa as *Faultless to a Fault*.

IV

In the present book, the second chapter starts with an external criticism against the *upamāna* as it is mentioned in the scheme of *pramāṇa*s by Gautama, the *sutrakāro*. The objection is external in the sense that the objection is not in relation to the nature of *upamāna* or whether it is to be accepted as an independent *pramāṇa* or not, etc. The objection is external also in the sense that the scheme of *pramāṇa* by including *upamāna* in the third position of the string made the scheme of *pramāṇa* anomalous, thus becoming a weak scheme of *pramāṇa*. It would have been better if Gautama could discard *upamāna*. In that case, scheme was to come only of three *pramāṇa*s like perception, inference and *śabda*. But as insertion of *upamāna* is not from emotional necessity and it depends on logical necessity, I have taken the hard task for showing the consistency of the scheme of four *pramāṇa*s like *pratyakṣa*, *anumāna*, *upamāna* and *śabda*.

In the third chapter, I have considered another objection which may also be called external objection. This objection comes from the fact that the reader may ask why the Nyāya and Mīmāṁsā schools are so much inclined to debate regarding the nature and status of similarity (*sādṛśya*). This is the concept where philosophers are only taking interest for various reasons.

However, it has no specific importance in science or in ordinary life. So the concept is insignificant. So in the chapter I have taken care to show how much the concept of similarity is important in science and in ordinary life.

In the fourth chapter, the Mīmāṁsā position relating to *sādṛśya* is shown and then is shown the weakness of the Mīmāṁsā thesis. Gaṅgeśa has discussed and established to the Navya-Nyāya position regarding *sādṛśya*. He has shown that *sādṛśya vyabahāra,* i.e. usage of similarity is valid but *sādṛśya* as an independent category is not acceptable. Gaṅgeśa has shown that *sādṛśya* is reducible to some other category. Accordingly, in relation to Mīmāṁsā position, Gaṅgeśa's stand is getting favour from law of parsimony. Gaṅgeśa has shown that *upamāna* can be admitted by admitting *sādṛśya vyabahāra,* i.e. usage of *sādṛśya*. But for that there is no need to admit *sādṛśya* (similarity) as independent irreducible category.

In the fifth chapter, it has been shown that *upamāna* is to be accepted not to explain the knowledge of similarity but it is important to have the knowledge of meaning relation in a particular context. Moreover, the *pramāṇa upamāna* is an irreducible independent *pramāṇa*, other than the three *pramāṇa*s, viz. perception, inference and testimony. The thesis relating to *upamāna pramāṇa* is faultless. It is only for some reasons or other, some philosophers could not give attention to this *upamāna pramāṇa*. But all the stalwart philosophers of the Nyāya tradition – Gautama, Jayantabhaṭṭa, Udayanācārya and Gaṅgeśa – have given much importance to this *pramāṇa* and made this *pramāṇa* at par with the other *pramāṇa*s. In the recent time, even Pandit Badrinatha Shukla in his unpublished paper defended this Nyāya theory of *upamāna pramāṇa*. So we cannot deny or ignore this *pramāṇa* from the Nyāya scheme of *pramāṇa*s. Gaṅgeśa's contribution is to make the defence with a height of perfection. I am not to claim that it is a final decision; one can again open the dialogue and it may continue but that will again draw our attention to the importance of this *pramāṇa upamāna*.

2

First External Objection

Anomalous Nyāya Scheme of Pramāṇas

I

In my previous book, *Dishonourned by Philosophers: Upamāna in Indian Epistemology*, I have defended the position of the Nyāya school regarding the admission of *upamāna*. So it can be said that I have honoured *upamāna*, a neglected *pramāṇa* by all the different schools of Indian tradition. Only the Mīmāṁsakas, other than the Naiyāyikas admitted this *upamāna*; of course, that is also in a different sense of *upamāna*. The Naiyāyikas admit *upamāna* for the knowledge of word–meaning relation while the Mīmāṁsakas admit *upamāna* for the knowledge of unperceived similarity. In my previous book, I have shown the exact difference between Nyāya and Mīmāṁsā regarding the nature of *upamāna*. But there I have taken only in a limited way the Mīmāṁsā criticism against the Nyāya. I have given much importance to the criticisms of the Bauddhas and Vaiśeṣikas. I have defended the Nyāya position against the Vaiśeṣikas and also against the Bauddha view. Indeed, my final position was stated following the eleventh-century philosopher, Udayanācārya. At that time the stronger opposition of the Nyāya school was from the Mīmāṁsakas, an *āstika* school of Indian philosophy. The Mīmāṁsā school is *āstika* (believer of the Vedas) and at the same time being a realist and a pluralist. In the same way the Naiyāyikas are also *āstika*s, realists and pluralists. Both of them admit *upamāna* but absolutely in two different senses. So if we want to establish the Nyāya position, we need not only to discard the views of Bauddha and Vaiśeṣika but also need to show that Mīmāṁsā position is also untenable. In his monumental work *Tattvacīntāmaṇi* Gaṅgeśa has done the same. He has shown that the Mīmāṁsā position on *upamāna* is also untenable. In this book, my main objective is to analyse the Mīmāṁsā position and how Gaṅgeśa has criticized the Mīmāṁsā view of *upamāna*.

Earlier I had considered the theories of *upamāna*, which involves definition or process or the result, etc. of *upamāna*. Accordingly the criticisms of Bauddha and Vaiśeṣikas were against the validity of *upaṃāna* or independence of *upamāna* in relation to the other *pramāṇa*s. All these criticisms can be named as a kind of internal criticism. Criticisms are internal in the sense, they are against the existence of *upamāna*. But in the literature we find some external objections as well. The external objections consist in raising the question regarding the status of *upamāna*. With reference to the previous book it can be stated that even if *upamāna* is an acceptable *pramāṇa* for certain kind of knowledge of word–meaning relation, yet *upamāna* is not to be accepted as per with the other three *pramāṇa*s so it is not to be mentioned in the list of the four *pramāṇa*s, viz. *pratyakṣa*, *anumāna*, *upamāna* and *śabda*. More precisely it is to be stated that the insertion of *upamāna pramāṇa* in the list or scheme of *pramāṇa* makes the Nyāya scheme anomalous. Introduction of *upamāna* to the Nyāya scheme of *pramāṇa*s creates really a great problem. Therefore it is of no use to admit *upamāna* in the Nyāya philosophy. Nobody should admit anything because it can create a problem. A Naiyāyika can say that *upamāna* has to be admitted for it explains one type of knowledge. But then a Naiyāyika should say that there is good reason to admit *upamāna*. And there is also good reason to drop *upamāna*. This is a paradoxical situation. It is like the situation which the scientists face. W.V.O. Quine has shown that scientists cannot do without the concept of similarity. But this concept is scientifically repugnant. What scientists can do?

Quine has solved this paradox. Similarly, a Naiyāyika must find a solution to the problem which arises because *upamāna* must be admitted and yet *upamāna* creates a problem. We shall try to solve this problem. We shall first state and explain the problem. Then we shall solve it.

The problem in question is that the Nyāya scheme of *pramāṇa*s, which contains four *pramāṇa*s, is anomalous. This scheme becomes anomalous if *upamāna* is admitted. If we drop *upamāna* and keep only three *pramāṇa*s then the Nyāya scheme is not anomalous. What we mean is this: if more than one *pramāṇa* is admitted, then the relation between the *pramāṇa*s must be explained. The Naiyāyikas or Gautama (1985: 1.1.3) admitted four *pramāṇa*s. But the Naiyāyikas cannot make clear the relation between these *pramāṇa*s. So the Nyāya scheme is anomalous. Uddyotakara first raised this question. He tried to solve this question also. But generally the Naiyāyikas do not discuss this question. In the writings of many Naiyāyikas, particularly in Gaṅgeśa, we find some hint how this problem may be solved. But following these hints also we cannot easily solve the problem if there are four *pramāṇa*s, or if *upamāna* is also admitted in the scheme of four.

Uddyotakara formulated the question in the following way. There are four *pramāṇa*s (special means of knowledge). What should be the order (*krama*) among them? Gautama in his *sūtra* admitted them in this order, *pratyakṣa* (perception) in the first place, *anumāna* (inference) second, *upamāna* (analogy) third and last, *śabda* (verbal testimony). But what is the principle behind admitting this order? Some acceptable principle should be shown to support this ordering. Our discussion of the Nyāya theory of *upamāna* will be incomplete if we do not discuss the place of *upamāna* in the total scheme of *pramāṇa*s of the Naiyāyikas. How is *upamāna* related to other *pramāṇa*s in the Nyāya scheme of *pramāṇa*s?

It is more important to note that if the relation of *upamāna* to the other *pramāṇa*s cannot satisfactorily be answered then the Nyāya scheme will be anomalous. If the introduction of *upamāna* makes the Nyāya scheme anomalous, then it is useless to admit *upamāna*. Thus one argues that *upamāna* is useless because *upamāna* makes the Nyāya scheme incoherent or inconsistent. Again if the relation of a thing to other things cannot be made clear, then the nature of that thing must be doubtful.

II

Uddyotakara in his *Nyāyasūtra-Vārttika* (1985: 91) has considered more than one view. He has considered more than one way of justifying the order or relation of the *pramāṇa*s. According to one of the views following is the justification for placing *upamāna* after *pratyakṣa* and *anumāna*, and before *śabda*. Gautama enumerated *pratyakṣa* first because it is the most basic or most important (*prādhānyāt*). He placed inference after perception because inference depends on perception (*tatpūrvakatvāt*). Analogy has been enumerated next for it resembles *anumāna* (*tatsādharmyāt*). *Śabda* (verbal testimony) has been placed last because it gives us knowledge of all objects or greatest range of objects (*mahāviṣayatvāt*).

Against this view or explanation we have two objections. First, it is not clear what is meant by *tatsādharmyāt*. For if *upamāna* resembles *anumāna*, then *anumāna* also resembles *upamāna*. So according to this principle it will be right if one enumerates *anumāna* after *upamāna*. We shall see that Gaṅgeśa has given a better answer. Second, this defence of Gautama's way of ordering *pramāṇa* appears to be ad hoc. In case of each *pramāṇa*, there is a different principle. No single principle of ordering has been followed. This shows that Gautama's scheme of *pramāṇa*s is anomalous or incoherent. Moreover, it violates the law of persimony.

Uddyotakara considered in his *Vārttika* a second view or explanation of the order of the four *pramāṇa*s. According to this view, nobody can utter the names of the four *pramāṇa*s at once. That is physically impossible. According to this view, therefore, the *pramāṇa*s must be introduced one after another. It is a matter of physical necessity. Against this explanation it can be said that the explanation is unacceptable for two reaons. First, this view explains why the *pramāṇa*s should be enumerated (their names should be uttered or written) one after another. But it has not explained why *upamāna* should be enumerated after *anumāna* and not before or after *pratyakṣa* or before *anumāna* or after *śabda*. Second, we are discussing a different question. We are not discussing the question whether the *pramāṇa*s should be enumerated or written one after another. The question we are discussing is the following:

> Is there any objective relation among the *pramāṇa*s, is there any single principle, which can justify the order of the *pramāṇa*s which Gautama has shown in his *Nyāya-sūtra*, 1.1.3?

This question has not been answered at all.

We have already considered the first view or explanation and found it unacceptable. Uddyotakara has also criticized it. He has said many things. But we shall here note only a few of them. He has shown that principle *mahāviṣayatva* holds both about *śabda* and *pratyakṣa* (perception). So this principle cannot justify the last position of *śabda*. *Pratyakṣa* can also be given that position. Again why should a *pramāṇa* which has *mahāviṣaya* be placed last? It could be a good reason to give a *pramāṇa* the first position. For a *pramāṇa* which knows all or most of the things is superior to other *pramāṇa*s which know less number of things. But how can Uddyotakara say that perception is *mahāviṣayavān*? From *śabda* we know present and future objects. But perception can give us knowledge of some present objects only. Uddyotakara has a very clever answer. He says that all the things of the world can be grouped into three classes: the universal, the particular and that what has the universal. And perception can know *jāti vyakti* (separately) and a complex thing (*viśiṣṭa viṣaya*) which is not a mere particular or a mere universal, but a particular qualified by universal. We can give an example. In *nirvikalpaka pratyakṣa*, we know separately a universal and a particular. But in *savikalpaka jñāna*, we know a *viśiṣṭa viṣaya*.

The more important thing which Uddyotakara has shown is this. We do not need both the principles *prādhānya* and *tatpūrvakatva*. For he says all the *pramāṇa*s (other than *pratyakṣa*) are *pratyakṣa* (*tat*) *pūrvaka*. But if all the *pramāṇa*s are causally dependent on *pratyakṣa*, then *pratyakṣa* should be the first and all other *pramāṇa*s should come after *pratyakṣa*. So we do not need in addition to the principle of *tatpūrvakatva*, as the principle of *prādhānya*. The supporters of the first view may take this hint from Uddyotakara and reduce the number of principles from four to three – *tatpūrvakatva*, *tatsādharmya* and *mahāviṣayatva*. Because all the other *pramāṇa*s depend on *pratyakṣa* (*sarvapramāṇānām pratyakṣapūrvakatvāt*), Gautama is justified to place it first in the list of *pramāṇa*s. But *anumāna* must come before *upamāna*. For *upamāna* has resemblance with *anumāna*. And *śabda* must come last because it is *mahāviṣaya*. It gives us knowledge about which other *pramāṇa*s produce knowledge; and it gives us knowledge of some more things.

But our objection against the first view still remains valid. It cannot discover any single principle on which the order of all the *pramāṇa*s can be based. Vācaspati Miśra in his *Tātparyaṭīkā* (1985: 91) has noted one argument to support the number one position of *pratyakṣa*. This argument was originally given by Vātsyāyana (1985: 92). It has been said by Vātsyāyana that *pratyakṣa* is the most superior among all forms of knowledge. It is immediate and direct. It puts an end to all doubts.

Many years later Gaṅgeśa said explicitly in his *Anumānacintāmaṇi* (1970, II (I): 1) that *anumāna* has been placed after *pratyakṣa* because *anumāna* depends causally on *pratyakṣa*. This is an old and familiar justification of the order, first *pratyakṣa*, then *anumāna*. Even at the time of Gautama, this argument was known. Vācaspati Miśra had clarified the point. He said that we may find examples of inference which depend not on *pratyakṣa* but on another inference or verbal testimony. But Vācaspati Miśra said that ultimately every inference is dependent on perception. Long afterwards Raghunatha Siromani noted a case of *pratyakṣa* which causally depends on *anumāna*. But if *pratyakṣa* is *anumānapūrvaka*, then *anumāna* should come before *pratyakṣa*. But Raghunatha (1970: 6-7) also showed that there is a difference. All inferences causally depend on *pratyakṣa* (or is *pratyakṣapūrvaka*). But only some perceptions are caused by inference.

Naiyāyikas from Gautama to Gaṅgeśa used the principle of causal dependence to justify the relative position of *pratyakṣa* and *anumāna* in the Nyāya scheme of *pramāṇas*.

III

We saw that the principle of causal dependence has an important relation between *pratyakṣa* and *anumāna*. On the basis of this relation, inference is placed after perception in the Nyāya scheme of accredited sources. But can we say that the relation of *upamāna* to *anumāna* is the same? We cannot say that. Why then *upamāna* is enumerated after *anumāna*? Uddyotakara notes the view that *upamāna* resembles *anumāna*; so *anumāna* is placed before *upamāna*. But what is the point of similarity between the two? Vācaspati Miśra (1985: 91) tells us that both analogy and inference depend on memory. *Anumāna* depends on memory of *vyāpti*. *Upamāna* (*upamiti*) depends on the memory of the content of the statement of analogy. But if both are dependent on memory, then why *upamāna* is placed after *anumāna*, and not *anumāna* after *upamāna*? Vācaspati Miśra has given an answer. He says inference depends on perception and memory. But analogy depends on perception, memory and verbal testimony (*atideśavākya*) (ibid.). But *upamāna* should be placed not only after *anumāna* but also after *śabda*. So we cannot explain the relation between analogy and inference in this way.

Gaṅgeśa gives a different justification. He says in his *Anumānacintāmaṇi* that *anumāna* is *bahuvādisammata* but *upamāna* is not *bahuvādisammata*. Everyone who admits *upamāna* admits *anumāna* also. But there are philosophers who admit *anumāna* but not *upamāna*. Bauddhas and Vaiśeṣikas are such philosophers. We have three objections against this defence. First, this principle of "acceptance by more people" (*bahuvādisammatatva*) can also explain why *anumāna* should be listed after *pratyakṣa*. Every philosopher who admits *anumāna* admits perception also. But the Cārvākas accept *pratyakṣa*, they do not accept *anumāna*. Now if this principle can explain the place of *pratyakṣa* and *anumāna* in this order then we do not need the other principle, *tatpūrvakatva*. Gaṅgeśa has accepted both the principles. This is unnecessary. Second, even if we drop the principle *tatpūrvakatva*, the Nyāya scheme remains anomalous. For one more principle will be required to explain the relation between *upamāna* and *śabda*. We cannot say that more people admit *upamāna* than *śabda*. But *śabda* has been listed after *upamāna*. Philosophers like Bhāsarvajña do not admit *upamāna*. But they admit *śabda* (Bhāsarvajña 1968: 79). Sāṁkhya philosophers also do not admit *upamāna* but admit *śabda*. There are no philosophers who admit *upamāna* but do not accept *śabda*. So according to the principle of *bahuvādisammatatva*, *upamāna* should be admitted after *śabda*. Some Mīmāṁsakas actually list *upamāna* after *śabda* (or *śāstra*) (see Parthasarathi 1913). If the Nyāya scheme of *pramāṇa*s is to be supported, then we need a second principle which can justify the place of *upamāna* before *śabda*. No single principle can explain the order of all the four *pramāṇa*s. So the scheme is anomalous. Third, two principles which Gaṅgeśa has actually used are completely different in kind. *Pratyakṣa* and *anumāna* are related as cause and effect. It is an important and objective relation. And the relation is asymmetrical. Cause always comes first and before the effect. But the principle *bahuvādisammatatva* is not equally important and objective. And there is no rule that what is *bahuvādisammata* must come first. It is only practically convenient to discuss first what more people accept. For then, we cannot say that *anumāna* comes before *upamāna*.

IV

One may suggest that the anomaly in the Nyāya scheme is due to *upamāna* or analogy. *Upamāna* creates all problems. If we omit *upamāna* from the list of *pramāṇa*s, then the order among the other three *pramāṇa*s can be explained by one single principle *tatpūrvakatva* or *upajīvya-upajīvakabhāva sambandha*. In other words, the single principle of causal dependence can support the order in which *pratyakṣa*, *anumāna* and *śabda* have been listed. *Anumāna* causally depends on perception. For *anumiti*, perception of *vyāpti* is necessary ultimately. Again perception of *hetu* is necessary. Similarly *śabda* causally depends on *anumāna*. For sentence alone can be *śabda pramāṇa*. And a hearer can derive knowledge from a sentence if he already knows the meaning of the words of the sentence. Word-meanings can be known in many ways. The most basic among these ways is *vṛddha vyavahāra*. And this is actually inference. Thus one must first learn the word meanings from inference. Then if he hears a sentence containing these words, then he can remember the word-meanings. Then he can have *śabda-jñāna* about the relation of these word-meanings. In this way, *śabda* is also causally dependent on inference.

If *upamāna* is dropped from the Nyāya scheme of inference, then the scheme becomes consistent and rational. One single principle of causal dependence can explain the order of the *pramāṇa*s: first perception, then inference and then verbal testimony. But if *upamāna* is added to this scheme, the scheme becomes again anomalous. It must be placed after *pratyakṣa*. For it causally depends on *pratyakṣa*. But *pratyakṣa* does not causally depend on *upamāna*. It cannot be placed either before or after *anumāna*. For *upamāna* does not causally depend on *anumāna*.

Anumāna also does not causally depend on *upamāna*. But if *upamāna* cannot be placed after *anumāna*, it cannot be placed before *śabda*. For *śabda pramāṇa* presupposes prior knowledge of word-meanings. But word meanings can be known from other means and not from *upamāna*.

In this way introduction of *upamāna* makes the Nyāya scheme anomalous. If it is dropped then the Nyāya scheme becomes coherent. So it is useless to admit *upamāna*. *Upamāna* can give us the knowledge of word-meanings or word–meaning relation. This knowledge is necessary for *śabda pramāṇa*. But this knowledge can be derived from other sources. It can be derived from inference. And inference is the first and basic way in which word meanings are known.

This is one suggestion how Nyāya scheme of *pramāṇa* may be made consistent. The suggestion is to drop *upamāna*. This suggestion is made after already accepting that the introduction of *upamāna* makes the Nyāya scheme anomalous. No one from Gautama to Gaṅgeśa could give a satisfactory defence of the scheme of all the four *pramāṇas*. So *upamāna* creates more problem. If the present suggestion is accepted, then the Nyāya scheme will have only three *pramāṇas*. This scheme will be coherent and consistent. There will be no loss. Word-meanings can be known from inference. It cannot be said that if a scheme contains only three *pramāṇas*, it cannot be a Nyāya scheme of *pramāṇas*. For Bhāsarvajña was a Naiyāyika. He admitted only three *pramāṇas* by rejecting *upamāna*.

One may, however, think that the suggestion to drop *upamāna* and make Nyāya scheme consistent thereby is unacceptable. It is unacceptable for two reasons. First, if the suggestion is accepted, then it will be shown that Gautama's scheme is still defective. For one can then argue in the following way. If all four *pramāṇas* are admitted, no uniform explanation of their order can be given. So if we retain all the four *pramāṇas*, Gautama's scheme becomes anomalous. If we can drop *upamāna* then it is proved that Gautama admitted this *pramāṇa* without any necessity. He included in his scheme more *pramāṇa* than were necessary. It is a defect to admit more than what are necessary. Thus if we can drop *upamāna,* then that will show that Gautama's scheme or Nyāya scheme is defective. The second reason why we cannot accept the suggestion is this. *Upamāna* serves some purpose. Therefore even if *upamāna* creates some problem it serves some purpose and it is irreducible to any other *pramāṇa* also. How can we drop it? We can drop it if we can show independently that it is useless.

We think that Gautama has not admitted too many *pramāṇa*s. *Upamāna* is useful. And some satisfactory explanation of the order of all the four *pramāṇa*s may be found. We shall suggest one such explanation. But before that we must state another criticism against the Nyāya scheme or Gautama's scheme of *pramāṇa*s.

Let us take for granted that *upamāna* is useful. And satisfactory explanation of the order of all the four *pramāṇa*s can be given. In that case, the scheme of *pramāṇa*s may be exactly what Gautama has given us. But still *upamāna pramāṇa* differs importantly from all the other *pramāṇa*s. Gautama's scheme does not, however, show this. Gautama has enumerated all the four *pramāṇa*s together. So it confuses us. We may think that *upamāna* is just like any other *pramāṇa*. But it is not so. Other three *pramāṇa*s can prove the existence or non-existence of things. They are *padārthasādhaka pramāṇa*s. They prove *bhāva* or *abhāva*. If we are to accept a thing (called *paramāṇu*) or if we are to accept the *abhāva* of a thing (for example *śabde nityatvābhāva*), then we are to depend on these three *pramāṇa*s. *Upamāna* is not *padārthasādhaka*. It cannot prove the existence or non-existence of anything. The Naiyāyikas admit this great difference of *upamāna* from other *pramāṇa*s. But this is not clear from the way Gautama has enumerated all the *pramāṇa*s together. On another occasion, however, he did not enumerate all the items together. He admits six *indriyas* (sense-organs). But when he enumerated the *indriyas* he only listed the first five. Vātsyāyana in his commentary said that Gautama did this because he wanted to draw our attention to the fact that the sixth *indriya* or *manas* is very much different from the other five. We think that Gautama could do the same thing here also. If he did, then the things could be more clear.

Now, this becomes important to see whether the scheme is explainable by one principle. The most important principle of causal dependence can be used. This principle has been used by the Naiyāyikas from Gautama to Gaṅgeśa. We do not claim that the explanation we offer here was in the mind of Gautama and other Naiyāyikas. It may not be the only explanation. But this can also be an explanation. We shall not repeat the explanation why *anumāna* must be after *pratyakṣa* and *śabda* must be after *anumāna*. We accept that in terms of causal dependence *pratyakṣa*, *anumāna* and *śabda* come one after another. We shall try to defend in terms of causal dependence the place of *upamāna* between *anumāna* and *śabda*. If we remember the detailed explanation of the Nyāya theory of *upamāna*, it will be easy to follow the explanation.

First we need to see the steps of the process of analogy. Let us take the concrete case of *go-gavaya*.

Steps outside the given case:

(a) The city dweller asks the question *kīdṛk gavaya*? (How is a bison?)

(b) He is told by a forester who knows the answer *go sadṛśa gavaya*. "*Gavaya* is like a cow", i.e. bison is like a cow.

Steps of the actual process of a given *upamāna*:

1. The city dweller perceives in the forest an animal which is similar to cow.
2. The city dweller remembers the content of the statement of analogy (b) which the forester uttered.

3. The city dweller has the knowledge by analogy (*upamiti*) of the form *ayam gavaya padavācyaḥ* or "*gavaya gavaya padavācyaḥ*. "Yonder animal is a bison."

It is clear that for *upamiti* we need knowledge of similarity. We should have this knowledge twice, at the step (1) and before that at the step (b). Knowledge of similarity at step (b) comes from the understanding of the *atideśa vākya* (statement of analogy). In this statement there are two words *go* and *gavaya*. The city dweller does not know the meaning of the word *gavaya*. But he knows the meaning of the other word *go*. If he did not know the meaning of this word, then he could not be taught the meaning of the word *gavaya* by *upamāna*. For to be able to know the meaning of the word *gavaya* from *upamāna*, the city dweller must understand the words of the forester. The forester knows that the city dweller knows what a cow is. So the forester could tell the city dweller "*gavaya* is like a *go* (cow)". Now to learn the meaning of the word *gavaya* from *upamāna*, the city dweller must already know the meaning of the other word *go* which occurs in the statement of analogy. But this statement of analogy is a part of *upamāna*. A part of *upamāna* cannot depend on *upamāna*. Therefore the city dweller's knowledge of the meaning of *go* cannot be derived from *upamāna*. It must be derived from other means. Knowledge of *go* is necessary for understanding the *vākya* or *śabda* of the forester. Therefore the knowledge of the meaning of this word cannot be ultimately derived from *śabda*. It is ultimately derived from *anumāna*. Thus ultimately *upamāna* depends on *anumāna*.

Now let us take a case of *śabda pramāṇa*. A speaker says:

araṇye gavayāḥ santi (*gavaya*s live in the forest).

The hearer gets from this *śabda pramāṇa* the knowledge (*śabda-jñāna*) of the relation (*saṁsarga*) between the word-meanings (*padārtha*s). This is possible because the hearer can remember these word-meanings now. He can remember the word-meanings after hearing the words because he knew earlier what are the meanings of the words like *gavaya*. Now it is possible that the hearer learnt the meaning of this word from *upamāna pramāṇa*. Here *śabda pramāṇa* depends on *upamāna*. The nature of the dependence is causal.

We have seen that one can learn the meaning of the word by *upamāna pramāṇa* if he can understand the meaning of *atideśa vākya*. For *atideśa vākya* is a part of the process of *upamāna*. But one can understand in this case the meaning of the *atideśa vākya* if he already knows by other *pramāṇa* the meaning of the other word *go*. This other *pramāṇa* is ultimately *anumāna*.

Thus *śabda* depends on *upamāna* (at least in some cases) and *upamāna* depends on *anumāna* (ultimately). And the nature of this dependence is causal. According to the principle of causal dependence, the order of the *pramāṇa*s must be *anumāna, upamāna* and *śabda*. So Gautama is justified when he lists the four *pramāṇa*s in the order of *pratyakṣa, anumāna, upamāna* and *śabda*. The Nyāya scheme is not anomalous. So the objection of anomaly of the scheme of *pramāṇa*s is logically unacceptable and *upamāna* is acceptable in its own place in the string of Nyāya scheme of *pramāṇa*s.

3

Second External Objection
No Use of Similarity Outside Philosophy

I

In this chapter, we are raising another objection against the theory of *upamāna*. The objection, in short, is that *upamāna* is of no use in actual life or outside philosophy. The theory of *upamāna* or knowledge by similarity is concerned with the nature, use and knowledge of similarity. Such a theory has no bearing on practical life or even in theoretical studies other than philosophy. It has no bearing on science. It has no value outside Indian philosophy and ritualistic studies.

It may be said that the force of this objection is doubtful. For everything need not have practical use or value in terms of its multiplication of use. If something is useful in an area of theoretical studies then we cannot say that that is useless. Philosophy or theory of interpretation or philosophical hermeneutics is an important branch of knowledge. If something has value in any of these fields, it is ultimately useful. For usefulness it need not have use in other areas of knowledge or in all areas of knowledge. Lastly, philosophies of different cultures are naturally somewhat different. If the Indian philosophers developed certain techniques or discovered some explanations these cannot be useless, even if their use in other areas is not clear.

The point of the opponent seems to be this. *Upamāna* involves similarity. Suppose this notion is really theoretically important. It will be reasonable to expect that this concept will prove useful in other branches of theoretical studies. The Indian philosophers found it useful to study all about similarity so seriously, because the concept is really important. And one test of its genuine importance is that its importance is generally recognized. This then is the force of the objection. If the value of similarity is generally recognized – recognized outside Indian philosophy and outside philosophy – then we can be sure that it has genuine value. The second point of the objector is the following. A concept deserves greater attention if it is found to be useful beyond the narrow limits of highly abstruse theory like philosophy. A concept which has its use in the daily and practical life of ordinary men as well as in science must be a concern of all.

Now we shall show that the use of similarity is not confined only to Indian philosophical theory of word-meaning. First, it is recognized to be useful also in some Western philosophical theory of word-meaning. Second, similarity is useful outside philosophy and in science. We shall illustrate these two points with the example of Quine's theory of science and natural kinds. I shall use mainly Quine's paper "Natural Kinds". It is included in Stephen P. Schwartz edited anthology *Meaning, Necessity and Natural Kinds*. My purpose is to illustrate with example the point that the use of analogy or similarity is not a concern merely of philosophers or Indian philosophers. So a single example seems sufficient. Moreover, I do not know any other single short paper which brings together so naturally and nicely all the three or four things: analogy, learning words, natural kinds and science.

In the next section I shall bring out the points of comparison between Nyāya theory of *upamāna* and Quine's views on natural kinds. Then in the second place I shall briefly state the major points of Quine's paper in question. In the third place I shall briefly indicate some differences between the views of the Naiyāyikas and that of Quine.

II

The Nyāya theory of *upamāna* is primarily a part of the theory of the ways in which we learn meaning of words. In actual practice, the Naiyāyikas illustrate their theory of word-meaning and learning of word-meaning with the example of general terms. But they admit many more types of words. I shall explain this point. Then I shall narrate in a general way some of the problems about natural kind and natural kind terms, with which some contemporary philosophers of the West are concerned. I shall next examine briefly different types of meaningful (substantive) expressions and some of the different ways of learning word-meaning. Then in the next section I shall state the major points of Quine's paper and indicate the comparison between Quine's view and the view of the Naiyāyikas. In the last section, I shall elaborate some of these points.

The Nyāya theory of *upamāna* is different in many ways from the Mīmāṁsā theory of *upamāna*. The Nyāya theory of *upamāna* is a part of philosophy of meaning. For it is one of the many ways of learning meaning. It is one of the *śaktigrāhaka*s. This is not true about the Mīmāṁsā theory of *upamāna*. The Mīmāṁsā theory of *upamāna* is not a part of the theory of linguistic meaning.

The Nyāya theory of *upamāna* is the theory about a way of learning word-meaning (*śakti*). This theory has behind it two important tenets of Nyāya philosophy. According to the first tenet, linguistic expressions can be broadly divided into two categories *vākya* (sentence) and sub-sentential linguistic expression (*pada*). According to the second tenet, only the *pada*s are meaningful expressions (*śakya*). A word or a *pada* causes in the hearer the memory of the *padārtha* (or the thing which is the meaning of the word). A *vākya* gives us non-recollective awareness (*anubhava*) of the relation between some *padārtha*s. This relation is called *vākyārtha*. A *pada* stands to *padārtha* by the relation of meaning (primarily *śakti*). A sentence (*vākya*) stands to *vākyārtha* by way of *ākāṅkṣā*.

Gautama in his *Nyāyadarśana* has shown us a way of distinguishing a *pada* from a *vākya* (*sūtra* 2.2.58). He has also answered what are the meanings of a word (*sūtra* 2.2.66). He has said elsewhere (*sūtra* 2.1.55) that *śabdas* (words) can do their job because they bear the relation of *samaya* (*śakti*) to the corresponding things. *Sūtra* 2.2.58 of *Nyāyadarśana* is *te vibhaktyanatāḥ padaṁ*. It means those linguistic expressions (*śabdas*) are *padas* which have or take inflectional terminations. Sanskrit is an inflectional language. Words in it are always used with appropriate inflectional terminations. Thus a nominative expression (*nāma pada*) is always used after appropriate declension. Similarly only conjugated form of a verb word (*kriyāpada*) is used. For our purpose, it is important to note that a word is understood to have attached to its *vibhakti*. If a word is so understood, a sentence (*vākya*) can never be a word (*pada*). This shows that a Naiyāyika divides linguistic expressions (*śabdas*) into a *vākya* (sentence) and a *pada* (sub-sentential expression or word). It is also seen how these two types of *śabdas* can be distinguished.

Whenever we hear a particular word which is known, we recall a particular thing which we call its meaning. But how can a particular word recall a particular thing and not any other? According to Gautama, the basis of this regularity is the rule of the form:

> *asya śabdasya idaṁ arthajātam abhidheyamiti* ।
>
> – See Vātsyāyana 1985: 543

Vācaspati Miśra explains this with an example. He says God willed (*niyoga*) at the beginning of creation (*sargādau*) "the animal with dewlap (*sāsnā*, etc.) is alone the meaning of the word *go*". This rule which governs naming and named (*abhidhānābhidheya*) is called by Gautama *samaya* (see *Nyāya-Sūtra* 2.1.55 and Vātsyāyana's commentary on it). The important point for our purpose is that only words and the things which correspond to them come under this rule or relation of *samaya*. This *samaya* is the same as *vācya-vācaka-bhāva-sambandha* (Uddyotakara 1985: 544). We have seen so far that according to the Naiyāyikas words and sentences are different kinds of linguistic expressions. Second, the words alone are meaningful expressions. They alone have meaning. It, therefore, makes sense to ask the following question about words only:

(a) What does a word mean?

(b) How can we know what a word means?

It is almost customary for a Naiyāyika to illustrate these questions in the following way:

(a) What does a word like *gauḥ* (cow) mean?

(b) How can we know that (thing) the word *gavaya* means?

We shall soon see the implication of this. But before that we may discuss two points.

The first point is that every expression other than a sentence is a word in the broad sense. In this broad sense a word is any sub-sentential expression. But can we say that whatever is a word in this broad sense satisfies the criterion of Gautama? According to his criterion to be regarded as a word (*pada*), an expression must have *vibhakti* (inflectional termination or suffix) attached to it. But all sub-sentential expressions do not have *vibhakti*. We shall not discuss this point here. But Vātsyāyana has raised this question himself and answered it. We are mainly concerned here with more regular word forms like substantive or noun expressions. There is no reason to doubt that these words like *vibhakti* termination. The second point is the following. We have said that the question of learning meaning arises in the context of words. This problem is not a problem of Indian philosophy alone. In his book *Word and Object*, Quine has thoroughly discussed this question. There is one important difference. Quine like many other Western philosophers believe that the sentence is the primary unit of meaning. And in the matter of learning also, sentences are more central. We learn words usually in the context of sentences in which they occur. Learning a word is "learning, by example and analogy, the usage of sentences in which the word can occur" (Quine 1960: 13). But Quine also says that there is a good reason why "one usually speaks of learning a new word rather than a new sentence" (ibid.). He also says that there are a few types of words which may be learned but the learning of them cannot be said to be learning usage of sentences.

> It is mostly just substantives, adjectives, and verbs that will occasionally have been learned in isolation which of them is learned thus, and which only contextually, will vary from person to person. – Ibid.: 14

In any philosophy of language, Indian as well as Western criterion of words is an important question. But many contemporary Western philosophers believe that the distinction between word and meaning is not important. It is also believed that non-arbitrary criterion of word is not easy to give (ibid.: 13-14; also Harrison 1979: 51). In most of the Indian traditions the distinction between words and sentences is regarded as real and important. In different Indian traditions, different criteria of words have been given. Two most familiar criteria are the following. The standard view of the Vaiyākaraṇas is that a word is what takes *vibhakti* termination: *vibhyaktyantaṁ padam*. The other criterion of word (*pada*) is: a word is the bearer of meaning (*śakti*): *śaktyam padam*. This view of criterion is familiar as the Nyāya view of words. But Gautama is the founder of the Nyāya school. He has given as criterion of word what is familiar as the view of the Vaiyākaraṇas. Jayantabhaṭṭa, another Naiyāyika, has also defended this view. Some scholars think that what is familiar as the Nyāya criterion of word is actually Navya-Nyāya criterion. In the classical period there was no difference between the Naiyāyikas and the Vaiyākaraṇas.

It seems to us that Gautama's statement about words should be read in proper context. The *sūtra* in which Gautama stated the criterion follows his discussion on *varṇa*. The first word in the *sūtra* in question (*te vibhyaktantyāḥ padam* – 2.2.58) bears reference to these *varṇa*s. Therefore it seems that in the context of *sūtra* 2.2.58 Gautama's purpose was to distinguish *pada* from *varṇa* and the criterion stated in this *sūtra* serves this purpose. Moreover, by this criterion we can distinguish words from sentence (*vākya*) also. For sentences do not take *vibhakti*, only words take *vibhakti*. The objection against Gautama's criterion is that it excludes *vibhakti*s from words. But why that is objectionable? One may think if *vibhakti*s are not words, then *vibhakti*s cannot have meaning. This can be said only by those who have already accepted the other criterion – *śaktyam padam*. But for others there is no necessary connection between something having or not having *vibhakti* and something having or not having meaning. In the last place, it seems that there are two (or more) different ways or principles of division of *śabda*. One principle is whether a *śabda* has *vibhakti* attached to it or not. Another principle is whether a *śabda* has *śakti* or not.

III

Gautama and other Naiyāyikas believe that there is a real distinction between word and sentence. They also think that definite criterion of words can be given. The Naiyāyikas also think that regular association between (some) words and (some) things can be explained if we admit that words bear relation of *samaya* to things. Lastly, Gautama has also answered the question what are the things which a word means or refers to. The Naiyāyikas admit different types of meaning relation (*vṛtti*). The primary and direct meaning relation is called *śakti*. The indirect meaning relation is called *lakṣaṇā*. We shall consider here only *śakti*. How *śakti* (meaning or reference) is known? And how can we know what a word means? What a word means is called *padārtha* or *śakya* or *vācya*. And the *śabda*s which mean or name things are called *pada, śakta, vācaka* (or word).

The nominalists do not think that meaningful words have things corresponding to them. The Indian nominalists or

Buddhists "deny that there is some entity . . . that constitutes the own meaning of a word. . . . What is invariant about this word's semantic function" is what may be called *apoha* (Siderits 1991: 109). We shall not discuss this theory according to which there is no need to admit any real positive entity as meaning (*vācya*) of a word in isolation. Let us return to the question of meaning. According to the Naiyāyikas, meaning-relation (*vṛtti*) is of two kinds. But more important for our purpose is that there are different types of words also. There are not only nouns and verbs, there are *upasarga*s and *nipāta*s. But when the Naiyāyikas answer the question what is the thing which a word names, they almost always take words like cow (*gavaya*) (*Nyāya-Sūtra* 2.2.64). To draw attention to this fact, we re-write the question (a) as (a_1).

(a) What does a word mean?

(a_1) What does a word like *gavaya* mean?

Phanibhusan Tarkavagisa (1984, II: 495) has also tried to justify why Gautama discussed the word–meaning relation with reference to words which are names like *gauḥ*, *gavaya* and so on.

According to Gautama and other Naiyāyikas, a word means a particular thing (*vyakti*) as well as the universal character (*jāti*) and the peculiar physical structure (*ākṛti*) which the thing has. Gautama said *vyaktyākṛtijātayastupadārthaḥ* (2.2.66). When Gautama said this he had words like *go*, etc. in mind. What is the speciality about this type of words? Words of this type denote things which are substance of a certain kind. In other words, these types of words may be called natural kind words. In fact, what is said in the *sūtra* 2.2.66 can be strictly true about natural kind words (or a type). Śaṅkara Miśra says exactly this in his *Upaskāra* with reference to Gautama's *sūtra* 2.2.66. He says:

> *samayaḥ śaktireva vyaktyākṛtijātayaḥ padārthaḥ iti 'vṛddhāḥ gavādipadānāmiyaṁ gatiḥ, guṇakarmādivācaka-padānāntu jātivyakti evārtha iti. . . .* ।
>
> – Śaṅkara Miśra 1930: 190 on *Vaiśeṣikasūtra* 7.2.20

According to the Naiyāyikas, the words like *gauḥ* and *gavaya* are the representative or paradigm of meaningful words. These words name all the particulars of a kind which look similar because they have similar physical structure. These terms are species terms or natural kind terms. In contemporary Western philosophy, natural kinds and natural kind terms are very important topics of discussion. Discussions are often very technical and beyond the scope of this dissertation. I shall only summarize major points of Quine's paper "Natural Kinds". I shall show in that connection that the role of similarity in learning the meaning of natural kind terms is recognized by the Western philosophers. So even outside the Indian theory of *upamāna*, it is admitted that our knowledge of the meaning of certain words are knowledge by analogy. We learn meaning of words by similarity.

There are many problems relating to natural kinds as well as natural kind terms. Words (substantial expression) may be distinguished according to positions which they occupy in a sentence. So we have subject and predicate. From the point of view of modern logic, general names are predicates. Only proper names and singular terms can be subject. But how to clarify names for natural kinds? Should we treat them as general names or as proper names? Some philosophers think that proper names are disguised descriptions and so they are connotative. But other philosophers think that proper names are non-descriptional. The same truth is sometimes expressed by saying that things which proper names designate are not describable by means of language. We cannot describe Socrates by saying Socrates is a teacher of Alexander the Great. Such description does not give the meaning of the name of Socrates, i.e. "Socrates". We can teach the meaning of a proper name by pointing at the thing and uttering "This or he is Socrates". Now if we apply this criterion, then natural kind words like cow, tiger, lemon, etc. seem to be a kind of proper name. This is one easy way of introducing the problem of natural kind terms. Harrison 1979: 43 writes:

> Names for natural kinds can be learned before we learn any other names. . . . (We postulate the existence of natural kinds simply in order to have a way of explaining how language-learning could get started.) It follows that it is not necessary, in order to know the meaning of such a name *N*, that the natural kind which *N* designates should be characterizable or describable by means of language; except, of course, by means of such sentences as "This is an *N*", and so on. But now names for natural kinds begin to look . . . like proper name.

We select at random from a book the following arguments why natural kind terms like cow or tiger or *gavaya* cannot be descriptional. Take the case of single words or common nouns such as "tiger" or "cow" or "water" or "lemon". The term "cow" designates a kind or species, viz. the kind cow. Now if the term is to be descriptional, there must be some descriptions associated with it. It may be thought that (a) "being a cow" is that property. Others may dismiss it as a spurious description or property. They associate with a cow such property or properties as (b) being four legged, having dewlap (*galakambala*), etc. If one says that the term "cow" is descriptional because of the property (a) associated with it, then the term will be descriptional in a "trivial sense". If it is descriptional in terms of properties (b), then the term "cow" must apply to just those things which have (b). Some philosophers like Saul Kripke and Hilary Putnam think that descriptions and properties of the type (b) are important. But the properties of the type (a) are unimportant. Some critics say:

> Both Putnam and Kripke are prepared to allow that a natural kind term *V* may be said to be descriptional in terms of the alleged property denoting by "being a *V* . . . both seem to be suspicious of whether such alleged properties ought to be counted as genuine properties. Neither Putnam nor Kripke seem to give any cogent reason for countenancing some properties as playing an important role in the theory of

> meaning while dismissing such obvious properties as those of *being a lemon* and *being a tiger* as *ad hoc* and trivial.
>
> – Salmon 1982: 63; see also the quotation from Kripke in pp. 62-63

The Naiyāyikas are realists. They think that properties denoted by the expression "being a tiger" or "being a cow" (*gotva*) are very important. Normally they are objective universals and not *apoha* of the Buddhists.

According to Salmon, Putnam thinks that one may "explain the meaning" of a natural kind term such as "water" in an ostensive definition. Quine thinks that in our learning words by ostension, similarity plays an important role. This similarity is also involved in the notion of natural kind or in the explanation of the concept of natural kind. Thus Quine's theory is similar to the Nyāya theory of *upamāna*. According to both, the theories similarity and universal play important roles when we learn the meaning of words by analogy.

In the next section I shall briefly describe Quine's views. It can also show that there are important differences between the view of Quine and the view of the Naiyāyikas.

IV

We may summarize the major points of Quine's paper "Natural Kinds". Quine has shown three things: (A) A definition of similarity in terms of (natural) kind of definition of (natural) kind in terms of similarity becomes circular. He has also shown (B) that similarity cannot be accepted as an undefined and basic concept in any branch of science. The third thing that he has shown is (C) that in science we may and we do begin with similarity (or unconscious sense of similarity). Then as a particular branch of science develops the notion of similarity is gradually refined. And finally similarity is replaced by some of the fundamental concept of that branch of science. When Quine elaborated (B), he showed how important the concept of similarity is in natural science. (A) shows that similarity is a scientifically repugnant notion and (C) shows how (A) and (B) can be reconciled.

We are here concerned with two things. Quine has very clearly shown that similarity is a very useful notion in science and in practical life. He has also shown (B_1) that similarity is involved in learning language. It is particularly necessary in learning words through ostension. This has close similarity to learning the meaning of a word (i.e. *śakti*) through *upamāna*. We are also concerned with (A). Our point is that the Naiyāyikas do not define similarity in terms of kind or kind in terms of similarity. They, on the other hand, show that both similarity and kind (universal) are necessary. They are necessary in case of learning meaning of words (by ostension or) by analogy. Take the case of the word *gavaya*.

Gavaya is a natural kind like tiger. And, as Quine has shown, any two members of the extension class of a natural kind are more similar to each other. Any two *gavaya*s are closely similar to each other. One *gavaya* will be more similar to another *gavaya*. But if we take one *gavaya* and one camel (member of the extension class of the natural kind term "camel"), then they are more dissimilar. In terms of relative similarity, a *gavaya* is more similar to another *gavaya* and more dissimilar to a camel.

The Naiyāyikas have gone a step further. They will take three members from three natural kinds *gavaya, go* (cow) and *uṣṭra* (camel). A *gavaya* is more like a cow (*go*) than a camel (*uṣṭra*). So we must admit similarity (even relative similarity) between two members of the same natural kind and also two members of different natural kinds. Therefore, two things may be similar and still they may belong to different natural kinds. A *gavaya* and a *go* are similar. They are more similar to each other than they are similar to a camel. But similarity to a cow does not make a *gavaya* a cow. It still remains a *gavaya*. What then makes a *gavaya* a *gavaya*? The Naiyāyikas hold that we must admit the existence of what they call a *jāti* (genuine universal). Here it is *gavayatva*. It makes sense to say about a similarity that it is relative or absolute. But about a natural kind or universal, we cannot say it is relative. We can say about an individual animal (a *gavaya*) that is more similar to cows; it is less similar to camels. But we cannot say about a *gavaya* that it is more (of a) *gavaya*. We cannot say of an animal that it is less (of a tiger). An animal is either a *gavaya* or not a *gavaya*; either a tiger or not a tiger. Thus what makes an animal a *gavaya* is the universal property (*jāti*) *gavayatva*. A universal is the exclusive common property of the members of a natural kind. *Gavayatva* universal exists in all and only *gavaya*s. *Gotva* universal exists in all the members of the natural kind cow. It does not exist in anything else. But cow-similarity exists in *gavaya*s and in cows and perhaps in some other animals.

The Naiyāyikas, therefore, feel the need to admit in addition to similarity, universals. In our example, they admit both cow-similarity and *gavayatva*. Take any one *gavaya*. In it there are both the universal (property) *gavayatva*, and the (property) relative cow-similarity or *go-sādṛśya*. The Naiyāyikas next show that there is a central way of learning the meaning of natural kind words in which both these properties play their role.

The universal property *gavayatva* determines the exact scope or range of meaning (reference) of the natural kind term *gavaya*. The word *gavaya* applies to or refers to or mean all and only the *gavaya*s. In the idiom of Indian philosophy *gavayatvaviśiṣṭapiṇḍa gavayapadavācyaḥ*. It means an entity having the property of being *gavaya* (bison) "is the meaning of the word '*gavaya*'". The universal *gavayatva* is the *vācyatāvacchedaka*.

It is possible that a man is familiar with the word *gavaya*. It is also an objective fact that each and every *gavaya* has this property. And yet the man does not know what is the referent of the word *gavaya*; to which *thing* the word refers. Suppose the man has picked up the word *gavaya* from a dictionary.

Somewhere in the world there are animals which have *gavayatva*. But how do we know that the animal which has *gavayatva* is the referent of the word *gavaya*? How can we get the knowledge *gavaya* is *gavayapadavācyaḥ*? There are different means which give this form of knowledge. One of the ways of getting this knowledge may be described in the following way.

The man in our example may look up the dictionary to learn the meaning of the word. What will he find? He will find in the dictionary against the word *gavaya*, "an animal which resembles cows". But the man still does not know which is that animal which is "like a cow" (but not a cow). He later visits a zoo. He finds there a *gavaya*. That means he finds an animal which has the universal *gavayatva*. He also finds that this animal has cow-similarity. Because he knew from what he read in the dictionary, he can know that this cow-similar (*go-sadṛśa*) thing (*piṇḍa*) is the meaning of the word *gavaya*. What he read or heard enables him to recognize an animal as the referent of *gavaya* by noticing that the animal has cow-similarity. But the referent of the word is the animal *gavaya*. And an animal is *gavaya* (or belongs to the kind *gavaya*) because it has *gavayatva*. So he knows that the cow-similar animal (*prāṇī*), which has *gavayatva* is the referent of the word *gavaya*. *Gavayatva* enters as part of the meaning of the word. For *gavayatvaviśiṣṭaprāṇī* is the referent (meaning or *artha*) of the word *gavaya*. The property cow-similarity is associated with this *gavayatva*. So it is known as *upalakṣaṇa*. It is neither the *śakya* nor the *śakyatāvacchedaka*. It is no part of the meaning. But it can be a part of what we know when we know the meaning of the word as we were told *go sadṛśa gavaya*.

> *atropalakṣaṇatvamca tatpadajanya bodhaviṣayatvena śaktya-viṣayatvam* ।   – Bhimacarya 1978: 170

4

The Internal Defence
The Mīmāṁsā View and Its Limitations

I

In the chapter on *upamāna* of his *Tattvacīntāmaṇi*, Gaṅgeśa refined and defended the Nyāya theory of *upamāna*. For this purpose he has considered in detail the Mīmāṁsā view of *upamāna*.The methodology he has adopted is this. First, he has developed very strongly the Mīmāṁsā view; then he has discarded that Mīmāṁsā view from the standpoint of the old Naiyāyikas. He of course does not accept the view of the old Naiyāyikas. So finally he has also discarded the view of the old Naiyāyikas and established the view of the *navya* (neo) Naiyāyikas.

The Mīmāṁsā view of *upamāna* involves the notion of similarity.[1] So Gaṅgeśa has considered very closely the notion of similarity when he considered the Mīmāṁsā view of *upamāna*. Different problems are raised in relation to the notion of similarity. But here also Gaṅgeśa by discarding the view of the old Naiyāyikas and Mīmāṁsakas finally has established the view of the Navya-Naiyāyikas or particularly the view of the syncretic school.

The text *Upamānacintāmaṇi* starts with the sentence *athopamānam nirūpyate*, i.e. (after *anumāna*) *upamāna* is being investigated. Gaṅgeśa's discussion on *upamāna* is very difficult, particularly in the first part. I shall here try to follow his text

[1] Of course, the Nyāya view also involves this notion so far as *upamāna* is taken in the sense of instrumental cause of *upamiti*. But they do not hold that *upamiti* as the knowledge of *sādṛśya*.

closely. But I shall not translate the text but briefly state and explain the major points. I am doubtful whether I understand Gaṅgeśa's position clearly. *Upamānacintāmaṇi* has two major divisions. In pages 1 to 45, major topic of discussion is whether *sādr̥śya* is an additional category. In the rest of the book the major point of discussion is whether *upamāna* is an additional *pramāṇa*.

Gaṅgeśa, in his text, first states the view of the Prābhākara Mīmāṁsakas. In his elucidation, Krishnakanta Vidyavagisha (1990) writes:

> *sādr̥śyasya atiriktapadārthatāvādinām mīmāṁsakānām matam upanyasyati tatretyādinā*

It means that Gaṅgeśa's passage which begins with the word *tatra* is the view of those Mīmāṁsakas who hold that similarity is an additional kind of existent. And we are aware from our previous discussion that Prābhākara and his followers accept *sādr̥śya* is an additional category.

Gaṅgeśa first has given the Prābhākara definition of *upamāna* when he considered the Mīmāṁsā view of *upamāna*. The definition of *upamāna* is this. The instrumental cause of the non-recollective knowledge of similarity (P_1) (*sādr̥śya pramākaraṇaṁ upamānam*-P_7) is *upamāna*. In the second place, he states characteristically Prābhākara view about *sādr̥śya*, viz. (P_2) *sādr̥śyam ca padārthāntaram*. *Sādr̥śya* or similarity between things is an irreducible kind of entity. In his *Br̥hatī*, Prabhākara only rejected the view that *sādr̥śya* is *sāmānya* or universal.

> *atra sāmānyameva kaiścit sādr̥śyamuktam na tatsādr̥śyam*
>
> – Prabhākara 1934: 109

But he has not discussed there if *sādr̥śya* can be reduced to any other kind of thing. Śālikanātha Miśra (1961: 268) in his *Prakaraṇapañcikā* did that elaborately.

We have already mentioned that Gaṅgeśa has elaborately considered the Mīmāṁsā view of *sādr̥śya*. He first stated in page

7 of his *Upamānacintāmaṇi* that *sādṛśya* is an irreducible category (P_2). He then elaborately discusses this point. His discussion of this point covers some 38 pages of the Asiatic Society edition. He returns to the view (P_1), i.e. *upamāna* is the instrumental cause of the knowledge of *sādṛśya* (p. 45).

We know from our previous discussion that both Prābhākara Mīmāṁsakas and Bhāṭṭa Mīmāṁsakas agree on the point (P_1), i.e. *upamāna* is the instrumental cause of the knowledge of similarity. But the Prābhākara view that similarity is an irreducible category has been criticized both by the Bhāṭṭa Mīmāṁsakas and Naiyāyikas. Gaṅgeśa has considered the criticisms of the Bhāṭṭas and the Nyāya-Vaiśeṣika syncretic school. Of course, he has also said all that can be said against the Bhāṭṭas and Nyāya-Vaiśeṣikas from the side of Prābhākaras.

First, he has stated the Prābhākara view and offered considerations in favour of it. Then he has criticized the view. Now, according to the Prābhākaras, *sādṛśya* is a kind of thing of being. The Prābhākaras accept three important views regarding *sādṛśya*:

1. (P_2) *sādṛśya* is an irreducible category (*sādṛśyañca padārthāntaraṁ*) – p. 7
2. (P_3) *sādṛśya* exists (*astisādṛśyam*) – p. 7, and
3. (P_4) *sādṛśya* differs as its locus differs (*pratyāśrayaṁ bhinnaṁ*) – p. 11.

Among the three, the second point, i.e. P_3 is important. For we saw earlier that the rejectionists like the Bauddhas do not accept P_3. They think that there is no such thing as *sādṛśya*. Ratnakīrti argued that there was no *upamāna* because the object of it was not there (1957: 94).

He meant that there was no *sādṛśya*. So P_3 is a debatable or a controversial point. Prābhākaras are to offer argument we prove (P_3). Gaṅgeśa has done that. He has stated an argument from the side of the Prābhākaras. He says:

sādr̥śyavyavahārāt abādhitāt asti sādr̥śyam
– Gaṅgeśa 1990, III: 1[2]

It means there is *sādr̥śya* (similarity) because there are linguistic usages which are correct. Any usage or anything anyone says cannot prove that the thing spoken about exists. For example, we say "little star" or "twinkle twinkle little star". On the basis of this one cannot say that there is a little star. One cannot say that the stars are small in size. These usages are not correct. They are contradicted by sentences in science books or by what the scientists say. From the side of Prābhākara, Gaṅgeśa says that there are correct usages about *sādr̥śya*. People say that "*a gavaya* (bison) is like a cow" (*go sādr̥śya gavaya*). This statement of analogy is correct. Nobody says it is false. Many more correct sentences of analogy are there. So it follows that there is *sādr̥śya*. And accordingly Prābhākara is statement P_3 is true.

The Prābhākaras hold, in addition to P_3 and P_2, that P_4 is also true. P_4, as we have already stated, states that *sādr̥śya* or similarity differs when the locus becomes different. The point is that when two things resemble each other, *sādr̥śya* exists in each of the two things. But *sādr̥śya* which exists in the first thing is different from the *sādr̥śya* which exists in the second thing. So when we say that *gavaya* is similar to cow (*go*) then both *gavaya* and *go* have similarity. But the similarity that exists in *gavaya* is different from the similarity that exists in the *go* or cow:

sādr̥śyam bhinnam; anyadeva hi gavi gavaya sādr̥śyam; anyat ca gavaya gosādr̥śyam – Śālikanātha 1934: 109

The point is very important for the Mīmāṁsakas and Prābhākaras.

For according to them, the similarity that is there in *gavaya* can be known by perception. But for the knowledge of similarity that is there in *go* or the cow, we need another *pramāṇa* called

[2] Kumārila in his *Śloka-Vārttika* said: *sādr̥śyasyapi vastutvam śakyam apabādhitum* (*Upamāna Pariccheda*, verse 18).

upamāna pramāṇa. One may say that a separate *pramāṇa* called *upamāna* will be needed if we admit that *sādr̥śya* which exists in different loci are different or if P_4 is true. Gaṅgeśa shows elaborately how Prābhākaras can prove (P_4). It is very difficult to discuss all the arguments. So two major arguments here are taken to show the Prābhākara position.

The Prābhākaras say that if the same *sādr̥śya* exists in all the things that are similar, then P_4 will be false. But can the similarity in all the similar things be one and the same? The Prābhākaras say that this cannot be. For supposing *gavaya* and *go* are two similar things. So there is similarity in them. And as this similarity exists in them, we say that *gavaya* is like *go*. Now we also say and experience that the face of a certain girl is like the moon. So there must be similarity in the face and the moon. If it is the same similarity (that exists in *go* and *gavaya*), then the consequence will be this. The face will be like the *go*. In this way if everything which is similar to something had same similarity then everything would be similar to every other thing. To express this argument from the side of the Prābhākara Mīmāṁsakas, Gaṅgeśa writes:

> *tacca na pratipadārthamekaṁ sarvasya sarvasādr̥śatvāpatteḥ*
>
> – 1990, III: 8

It means similarity which is present in many objects will not be the same one. If once it is admitted, everything will be like every other thing.

The second major argument of the Prābhākaras is the following. If there was only one single similarity instead of different similarities in different things, then we could not have such experience as "X is more similar or closely similar to Y" or X is slightly similar to Z.

But we have such experience. So there cannot be one single similarity in different loci. There must be many similarities. To explain the point let us take an example. We all understand that there is a similarity between a cow and an ass on the one hand, and a cow and a camel on the other. Now the similarity which is there in a cow and an ass is more close than the similarity that is there in a cow and a camel. Now in our ordinary life, we make the difference by admitting the number of similarities between a cow and a camel. If similarity was one and the same in all these, viz. cow, camel and ass, how could we in that case make the difference of our different experiences? So we cannot explain such experience of close similarity or small similarity (*susadṛśamandasadṛśavyavahārasya tadekatve anupapatteśca* – Gaṅgeśa 1990, III: 8) if we say that similarity is one and the same even when its loci differ.

Gaṅgeśa here has given some defence in favour of the opponent. The defence he has given in terms of suggestive property (*vyañjaka dharma*). He has also examined whether *sādṛśya* may be taken as a *vyāsajyavṛtti dharma* like *saṁyoga*. Now one can explain how we can have experience of *susadṛśa* and *mandasadṛśa* even though *sādṛśya* is one. We can explain this by suggestive property (*vyañjaka dharma*). But finally Gaṅgeśa has shown that P_4 is to be accepted and accordingly in page 11 he states P_4 by the words: *kintu pratyāśrayaṁ bhinnaṁ*. That is *sādṛśya* is different according to its different loci.

But one objection has been brought against the view P_4. The argument can be stated in this way: if there was no single similarity and if similarity in its plurality were different in each case, then we could not have the knowledge of sameness (*anugata pratyaya*) in relation to such similarity. That means if similarities of different loci were different from each other then we would have to admit that similarities were different. And if similarities were different, then there would not have been knowledge of the form "similar" in all the cases of similarity.

Another objection has been raised. The objection is this. We could not learn the meaning of the word *sādṛśya* or the word cannot have any meaning. Let us explain the point.

When we take an example of individual man, how do we know the meaning of the word "man"? How do we know that the individual is called man? We say that the individual has manhood and the word "man" stands related by the relation of meaning to any thing which has manhood. Now we find Rāma has manhood and we learn Rāma is a man or Rāma is the meaning of the word "man". Suppose the manhood which has there in Rāma is not there in Lakṣmaṇa. Then we cannot know that Lakṣmaṇa is also a man; he is another meaning of the word man. Suppose manhood is different in each case. Rāma has manhood-I, so we learn that Rāma is the meaning of the word "man". If we say that Lakṣmaṇa does not have manhood-I, we cannot know Lakṣmaṇa to be the meaning of the word "man". Then it will follow that we cannot know the meaning of the word "man". The same is true with the word *sādr̥śya*. Suppose *sādr̥śya* is different in each case. We learn the similarity between a face and the moon. How can we know that what is there between a *go* and a *gavaya* is also similarity? How do we know that each is called similarity?

One may say that the similarities in the two different cases are really different. So there is no such question of knowing these two similarities as same. But if similarities are different in each case, then none of the similarities can be called similarity. We can have an experience of similarity in the absence of each of them. If manhood were different in all men, we could not call an individual person man. In the same way, we cannot learn the meaning of the word *sādr̥śya*. We understand this to be the point of the argument which has been raised against P_4, i.e. *sādr̥śya* is different according to its locus. In the words of Gaṅgeśa: *ekaikasya vyabhicārāt . . . . sādr̥śya padavyutpattiśca na syāt iti*. It means if *sādr̥śya* is used as one, then similarity and also the word similarity cannot be known.

Now it may be said that even if *sādr̥śya* is different in each case, yet we can know them all as *sadr̥śya* and can learn them as the meaning of the word *sādṛśya*. Take the case of hair. Each blade of hair is different from the other blade of hair, yet we experience them all as hair and know them as meaning of the word "hair". In the same way, let every similarity be different from every other similarity which exists in another *adhikaraṇa* or *āśraya* (locus). We can know them all as (similarity) *sādṛśya*, and so we can know the meaning of the word *sādṛśya*. Against this reply, it is said that the two cases are different. In case of hairs, we can have uniform experience and know them all as the meaning of the word "hair" because all the hairs have similar *ākāra*. They look alike. But different similarities do not have similar *ākāra*. So what is true about the hairs cannot be true about similarities.

Now Gaṅgeśa gives answer to the objections of the opponents from the side of the Prābhākaras. Similarities may not have the same *ākāra* and they differ as their loci differ. These statements are accepted by the Prābhākaras. But, according to the Prābhākaras, even then the experience of sameness can be explained. So in favour of the Prābhākaras, Gaṅgeśa (1990, III: 12) states *tayorupapatteḥ*. It means both uniform experience and (knowledge of) the meaning of the word *sādṛśya* will be possible. In the first place, similarity is admitted to be different in different instances. So there will be many different similarities. But all these similarities are experienced in the same way as "similarity". This shows that there is a thing like *sādṛśyatva*. Once such a property or thing is admitted we can see how there can be uniform experience of the form "similarity" and knowledge of the meaning of the word *sādṛśya*. We experience all the similarities in the same way, because they will have similarity-ness or *sādṛśyatva* (i.e. the property of being similar or *sādṛśya*). Again we can now see all those things will be the meaning of the word *sādṛśya* (similarity) which have *sādṛśyatva*. Thus the objections of the opponent of the Prābhākaras have been answered from the side of the Prābhākaras. And now accordingly from the answer of the Prābhākaras we can say that even when *sādṛśya* is different according to its different loci, yet by admitting *sādṛśyatva* we can explain both *anugata pratīti* and *sādṛśya pada vyutpatti* (knowledge of sameness and knowledge of the word similarity).

But this defence of Gaṅgeśa in favour of the Prābhākaras is not convincing. Because we know that the Prābhākara Mīmāṁsakas admit *jāti* only in substance. Such a *jāti* is *dravyatva*,[3] *ghaṭatva*, etc. If this is so, then what sort of thing is *sādṛśyatva*? If it is *jāti* then similarities will be *dravya*s. For, only substances have *jāti*. However, according to the Prābhākaras, *sādṛśya* is a different category of thing – different from substance, quality, etc.

Pragalbhācārya has given another argument, why a universal-like similarity-ness or *sādṛśyatva sāmānya* cannot be admitted. If *sādṛśyatva* is a *jāti*, then it will reside in all *sādṛśya*s (similarities). These similarities will be *jātimān*. But no *jātimān* (i.e. a thing that has *jāti*) can exist in *jāti* (Pragalbhācārya 1983: 3). So no similarity (or *jātimān*) can be in *jāti*. Then we cannot have such experience as *aśvatva* (horseness) is like *gotva* (cowness), for both are *nitya* – *yathā gotvam tathā aśvatvam*. But the Mīmāṁsakas admit that we have experience of similarity in case of universals or *jāti*s also.

Perhaps keeping all these in mind, Gaṅgeśa says that all that have been explained by, admitting *sādṛśyatva sāmānya* can be explained in other ways also. So Gaṅgeśa said *saptapadārthātiriktatvātvā* (1990, III: 12, see also Tachikawa 1981: 84-85 for other alternative) or, by the property of being other than the seven types of being admitted by the Vaiśeṣikas. These seven *padārtha*s are *dravya* (substance), *guṇa* (quality), *karma* (action), *sāmānya* (universal), *viśeṣa* (particularly), *samavāya* (inherence)

---

[3] *abhyupagamavādenoktam, pareṇa guṇādigata jāteranaṅgīkārāt iti bhāvyam* – Pragalbhācārya 1983: 3.

and *abhāva* (absence). We can know all the similarities in the same way and these similarities can be the meaning of the word "similarity", because they all have the property of being other than the seven categories of the Vaiśeṣikas. This reply is also unacceptable. For Navya-Mīmāṁsaka like Jaypuri Narayan Bhatta admits a ninth *padārtha* called *krama* (1961: 78). This *krama* has the property of being other than the seven categories of the Vaiśeṣikas. If the second reply is all right, then we will experience *krama* as *sādṛśya* and *krama* will also be the meaning of the word *sādṛśya*.

The third answer says that the case of similarities is like the case of *jāti*s. We can know all the similarities in an uniform way and all these similarities can be the meaning of the word "similarity". The explanation will be as in the case of *jāti*. There are any number of *jāti*s like jarness, manhood and so on. We know them all in the same way as *jāti*. We know all these are the meaning or reference of the word *jāti*. This is possible because all the *jāti*s have the same defining property (*lakṣaṇa*) which distinguishes all the *jāti*s from every other thing. One familiar definition of *jāti* is *nityatve sati aneka samavetatva* (Viśvanātha 1377: 51-52). It means *jāti* (universal) is eternal and resides in many in the relation of inherence. Another example where the presence of *lakṣaṇa* (or defining property) helps us to have uniform experience and knowledge of meaning is *viśeṣa*. *Viśeṣa* is the fifth category of the Vaiśeṣikas. There are indefinitely many *viśeṣa*s but all of them can be known in the same way as *viśeṣa*. And all of them can be the meaning of the word *viśeṣa* because they all have the *lakṣaṇa* of *viśeṣa*. One definition of *viśeṣa* which Udayana gave in his *Lakṣaṇāvalī* is:

> *samavetavattvarahitasarvānyonyābhāvasamānādhikaraṇa-samavetatvarahitasamavetā viśeṣāḥ* ।

This has been translated in the following way. Particularity inheres [in things], lack the property of inhering in the same loci as the mutual absence of all [its substrata], and lack the property of having that which inheres [in things] (Tachikawa 1981: 84-85). Thus the third reply comes to this. Though similarities are different from locus to locus (*pratyāśrayabhinnam*) and they are many, yet we can know them all in the same way as similarity. All these similarities can be the meaning of the word similarity. This will be possible because they have the same definition (of *sādṛśya*). This situation is similar to the case of *jāti* and *viśeṣa*:

> *jātivat antyaviśeṣavat ca svalakṣaṇāt vā tayorupapatteḥ*
>
> – Gaṅgeśa 1990, III: 12

So the point is this. Even if we admit that similarities are different according to their different loci, we can explain such *anugata pratīti* and also *pada vyutpatti*. So the Prābhākara position that similarity differs according to its locus is defended. Accordingly, we are to accept the Prābhākara position that *pratyāśraya bhinnaṁ sādṛśyam*. It means each similarity is different according to its locus where it belongs.

We now pass to the discussion of (P_3), i.e. similarity is an irreducible category (*atirikta padārtha*). The Prābhākaras admit this. But if a Prābhākara admits that *sādṛśya* is irreducible or *padārthāntara*, he is to explain what he means. If it is an additional *padārtha*, then what are the regularly accepted *padārtha*s? Is it meant that *sādṛśya* is additional to the number of *padārtha*s the Vaiśeṣikas accept? Or is it meant that *sādṛśya* is additional to the number of *padārtha*s the Bhāṭṭas admit? There is almost no difference between Navya-Bhāṭṭas and the philosophers of the syncretic school of Nyāya-Vaiśeṣika.

But in the classical literature of the Mīmāṁsā school when such problem whether *sādṛśya* is an additional *padārtha* was considered, it was generally understood whether *sādṛśya* was other than *sāmānya*. Perhaps the problem was so viewed in the context of Bhāṭṭa theory. The reason for so viewing may be this. There is a close similarity between *sāmānya* and *sādṛśya*. So if *sādṛśya* is to be reduced to any *padārtha* which a Bhāṭṭa accepts, it can be only *sāmānya*. The same seems to be true if one has the Vaiśeṣika scheme of *padārtha*s in mind. May be for this reason Prabhākara in his *Bṛhatī* raised the problem whether *sādṛśya* is a separate kind of being in this way:

> *atra sāmānyameva kaiścit sādṛśyamuktam; na tat sādṛśyam*
> – 1934: 109

In English translation it can be stated: in this context *sāmānya* is called *sādṛśya* but there is no *sādṛśya*. Thus Prābhākara has primarily in mind the view of those reductionist opponents who reduced *sādṛśya* to *sāmānya*, i.e. similarity to universal.[4] We find that Kumārila Bhāṭṭa in the chapter of *upamāna* of his *Ślokavārttika* has considered the view according to which similarity is equivalent to universal. He writes:

> *bhūyo 'vayava sāmānya yoga jātyantarasya tat*
> – 1978: 311, *śloka* 18

It means totality of the parts belonging in one class of objects. Gaṅgeśa also discusses in his *Upamānacintāmaṇi* whether *sādṛśya* is different from *sāmānya*. He examined the view of those who hold:

> *vijātīyatve sati avayava-guṇa-karma-vṛtti bhūyaḥ sāmānyam tat*
> – 1990, III: 15

We shall return to this question of reducibility of *sādṛśya* to universal in particular. But let us first discuss the position of the Vaiśeṣikas and philosophers of the syncretic school. These thinkers generally hold that the number of *padārtha*s (ontological categories) is only seven. These seven do not include *sādṛśya*

---

4 Here we notice a striking difference between the Indian and Western thinkers. In the West universal is reduced to similarity while in Indian tradition we see that similarity is reduced to universal. The debate as to whether similarity is an additional category is also peculiarly Indian.

as an independent category but according to them *sādṛśya* is reducible to these seven categories. Actually according to them anything, if it is a real entity, can be shown to be included in the seven categories. According to these Vaiśeṣika philosophers, *sādṛśya* is real as we have uncontradicted experience of *sādṛśya*. So they are ready to accept from the Prābhākaras that *sādṛśya* is to be admitted as we have uncontradicted experience of *sādṛśya*. But admission of the entity does not imply that it is an independent category. Neither it implies that it is not an independent category. So if the Vaiśeṣikas are to accept that *sādṛśya* is reducible category he is to show how *sādṛśya* is to be understood and to which of the seven categories *sādṛśya* may be reduced.

Udayanācārya who belonged to the Nyāya-Vaiśeṣika tradition demonstrated first that the Vaiśeṣika scheme of seven categories is correct. He accordingly showed that *sādṛśya* cannot be an additional thing; it cannot be other than these seven categories.[5] But Udayanācārya has done this at least twice. He did it in his *Pariśuddhi* (indirectly) on *Nyāya-Sūtra* 1.1.6. And again he did it in his *Nyāyakusumāñjaliḥ* (Udayanācārya 1967: 360 and 1957: 372f.).

In *Tattvacīntāmaṇi*, Gaṅgeśa has first reproduced Udayana's classification of *padārtha*s. Then from the Prābhākara point of view he criticized that the scheme cannot be accepted. I have discussed the argument of Udayana in my previous book. The argument shows that nothing can be other than or additional to the Vaiśeṣika categories. Take anything X (*sādṛśya, krama*, etc.) and a Vaiśeṣika will ask if X is a positive or a negative

---

[5] Gautama did not explicitly discuss Kaṇāda's scheme of six or seven categories. And Vātsyāyana seems to have already thought that there is no real difference between the Naiyāyikas and Vaiśeṣikas about the number of categories. So he has stated: *asti anyat api dravyaguṇakarmasāmānya-viśeṣasamavāyaḥ prameyam* – Vātsyāyana 1967: 382

entity. It cannot be both or it cannot fail to be any of the two. For *bhāva* and *abhāva* are logical opposites (*viruddha*). They are mutually exclusive and jointly exhaustive. Therefore only two alternatives for any X are there. It is either *bhāva* or it is *abhāva*. Now according to the Mīmāṁsakas, *sādṛśya* cannot be an *abhāva padārtha*. For the Prābhākaras do not admit *abhāva* as a category. So *sādṛśya* to be a *padārtha* must be *bhāva* (positive). But in the Udayanācārya way, *sādṛśya* cannot be an additional *bhāva padārtha*; additional to the six which the Vaiśeṣikas admit. Accordingly in the Udayanācārya way *sādṛśya* is not positive additional *padārtha satbhāva atiriktabhāva*. That means it is not a positive existent over and above the six recognized kinds of positive existents. It is reduced to one or more of these six *bhāva padārtha*s. It can be shown in this way after Udayana. If a *bhāva* thing has *guṇa*, then it is a substance or *dravya*. If it is not a seat of *guṇa*, then either it requires a locus or it does not require a locus. If it requires a locus (*āśrita*) and is characterized by an universal (*sāmānyavat*), and is of the nature of physical notion (*spanda*), then the X is nothing but what the Vaiśeṣikas call *karma*. If a *bhāva* thing does not have *guṇa*, has a locus, is characterized by universal, and other than *spanda*, then it is *guṇa* or quality provided it inheres in one locus (substance) only. If it inheres in many loci, then it is *jāti*. If an X is not a seat of *sāmānya* (*niḥsāmānya*) but inheres in some locus, then it cannot be *samavāya*. If such a thing inheres in one locus only it is *viśeṣa*. If it inheres in more than one (or in many), then it is universal. So from the point of view of Udayana, *sādṛśya* if it is a *padārtha*, it must be reduced to any one of these six *bhāva padārtha*s but *sādṛśya* cannot be an independent *padārtha*.

Gaṅgeśa here has raised objections from the side of the Prābhākaras, and at least against Udayanācārya. The objection is this. If the above argument is accepted, then it is to be accepted that even the last three *padārtha*s may also be reduced to the first three:

sāmānya-viśeṣa samavāyānām api dravyāditraya sādharmyāt-tattadantarbhāvaḥ – Gaṅgeśa 1990, III: 24

In the last case the Vaiśeṣikas are to admit that *padārtha*s are less than six or seven. That means this line of argument, which the Vaiśeṣikas bring against the Prābhākaras, goes against themselves. Because if we make the classification of *padārthas*, that can be done in different ways. We can do it in the previous way, i.e. by using the principle of *bhāvābhāva*. We may do the classification in some other way. We can argue in this way. Either a thing has *guṇa* or it does not have *guṇa*. If it has *guṇa* then it is *dravya*, otherwise it is *karma*. From this argument, it would follow that there would be nothing other than *dravya*, *guṇa* and *karma*.But this kind of reductionism shows that Vaiśeṣika reductionism is not acceptable. So by their scheme of categories, they cannot deny the irreducibility of *sādṛśya*. On the other hand, they are to accept the Prābhākara view that *sādṛśya* is an independent category.

Moreover, a Prābhākara can also say that the Vaiśeṣikas' approach is biased. They begin by assuming an ad hoc principle and use it to their own advantage. They declare anything unreal if the scheme based on this principle cannot accommodate it. It will be realistic if we argue in the other way. If we have experience of something, we are to accommodate that. If necessary we may have to revise the scheme of categories with which we begin. So we cannot say that *sādṛśya* is not a *padārtha* as the Vaiśeṣika principle or scheme is not able to accommodate this *sādṛśya*. So if Vaiśeṣika principle does not accommodate *sādṛśya* as an independent category, it is the fault of the principle rather than *sādṛśya*. *Sādṛśya* can as well be accommodated if we can use some other principle of division. This is the way in which Gaṅgeśa has shown from the side of the Prābhākaras why Udayanācārya's attempt to reduce *sādṛśya* is not acceptable.

Now let us grant that Udayanācārya's attempt is unacceptable. But how a Prābhākara can show that *sādṛśya* is an *atirikta padārtha*? We shall see how Gaṅgeśa argues in favour of the Prābhākara position. The point of the Prābhākaras is that *sādṛśya* is different from each of the seven types of things which the Vaiśeṣikas accept. In other words, we shall now present the positive argument of the Prābhākaras as has been stated by Gaṅgeśa. A Prābhākara may say that similarity resides in *guṇa* and *karma*. Therefore it cannot be any of the first three types of things which the Vaiśeṣikas admit:

> *tacca na dravyam guṇaḥ karma vā guṇakarma vṛttitvāt*
> – Gaṅgeśa 1990, III: 14

It means this. No substance or quality or *karma* (action) inheres either in quality or in action. But similarity is found in both of them. We say *gavaya* is like a cow. Here two substances are experienced as similar. We say colour of the rose is similar to the colour of the setting sun. Here two qualities (*guṇa*s) are experienced as similar. Again we experience the movement of an aeroplane as similar with the movement of a bird. This similarity is found to characterize substance, quality and action. But substance does not exist in quality or action; a quality (generally) does not exist in another quality or action; and an action does not exist in quality or action. Thus *sādṛśya* exists where substance, quality or action does not exist. Therefore *sādṛśya* is different from substance, quality and action.

This very argument could be used to prove that similarity is other than *viśeṣa* (Krishnakanta 1990: 23). It can be said that *viśeṣa* exists only in *dravya* while *sādṛśya* exists in all the three like *dravya*, *guṇa* and *karma*. Of course, Gaṅgeśa has not used this argument. Gaṅgeśa has offered another argument: *na viśeṣa pratyakṣatvāt* (1990, III: 23). It means this, *sādṛśya* is not *viśeṣa* as *sādṛśya* is perceptible. Gaṅgeśa obviously means by *pratyakṣa* ordinary perception of common man. For a section of scholars maintain that the *yogin*s can perceive in their extraordinary *yogaja pratyakṣa* or perception such differences as are caused by *viśeṣa*s:

tathā ca yoginām nityeṣu samānajāti-guṇa-kriyeṣu parāmāneṣu . . . yebhyo nimittebhyo vilakṣaṇa ayaṁ vilakṣaṇa ayaṁ iti vyāvṛtta dhī . . . te antyāḥ svāśraya viśeṣakatvāt viśeṣāḥ

– Pañcānan Śāstrī, 1377 (Baṅgābda): 64-65

This claim has however been challenged by some scholars. But there is no disagreement that *viśeṣa* is imperceptible if by perception we understand ordinary perception of common man. But though *viśeṣa* is imperceptible in this sense, similarity is not imperceptible. So a Prābhākara would say to a Vaiśeṣika that similarity cannot be reduced to *viśeṣa*. Gaṅgeśa also shows how a Prābhākara can prove that similarity cannot be reduced to what Vaiśeṣikas called *samavāya*. A *samavāya* does not inhere in anything but *sādṛśya* inheres in its locus. So Gaṅgeśa from the side of Prābhākara writes *na samavāyaḥ vṛttimattvāt* (Gaṅgeśa 1990, III: 23). Here *vṛttimattva* means *samavetatva* (*"Vṛttimattvāt" samavetatvāt* – Krishnakanta 1990: 23). It means *sādṛśya* (similarity) is not *samavāya* (inherence) as *sādṛśya* is *vṛtti* (exists) in the relation of *samavāya* in its locus.

But now the question is can *sādṛśya* be reduced to *sāmānya*? Gaṅgeśa shows how the Prābhākaras can argue that such reduction is not possible. We experience as similar not only two substances or qualities but also we sometimes experience two or more *jāti*s as similar. We have noted examples of experience where qualities are apprehended as similar. We also have such experience as the universal cowness is like horseness (for they are both eternal). We could not have these experiences unless similarities were there in *guṇa* (quality) and *sāmānya* (universal). But *sāmānya* does not exist in another *sāmānya*.[6] So *sādṛśya* is different from *sāmānya* also.

From the above discussion, we may note some special

---

[6] The *jātibādhaka* known as *anāvasthā* does not allow us to admit *jāti*s to have *jāti*.

features of *sādṛśya*. We shall also note some special features of our experience or usages about this *sādṛśya*:

1. We experience as similar things of the same kind (*sajātīya*) (*sajātiye 'pi aravindadvayavat* – Gaṅgeśa 1990, III: 17) and things of different kinds (*vijātīya*) (*visadṛśayoḥ karabha rāsabhayoḥ tat sattvāt ca* – ibid.: 18).
2. Similarity which exists in one locus is different from the similarity which exists in another locus:

   sāmānyāni āśrayabhedena abhinnāni bhavanti; sādṛśyantu bhinnam, – ibid.: 17

3. Similarity exists in *dravya, guṇa, sāmānya, viśeṣa* and *samavāya* also.
4. *Sādṛśya* is relative by nature. It is *saprativogika* like *sambandha* or *abhāva*. We just cannot say "similar". We would have to say "similar to . . ." something. So our experience of similarity is of the form "something is similar to some other thing(s)".
5. *Sādṛśya* is manifested when one becomes aware of the term or *pratiyogin* of the *sādṛśya*.

   sādṛśyantu sapratiyogikaṁ taddhīvyangyañca
   – ibid.: 21

6. *Sādṛśya* is experienced and reported (*vyavahāra*) as (a) *tat sādṛśya tena sadṛśa* or *tasya sadṛśa* but not as *tasmāt sadṛśa*; it is also experienced and reported as (b) more or less, i.e. *susadṛśa* and *manda sadṛśa* (cf. ibid.: 17, 21).

Most of the noted characteristics show, according to the Prābhākaras, that similarity cannot be reduced to *sāmānya*. More specifically the characteristics 2, 4 and 6 show that *sādṛśya* cannot be *sāmānya*. But philosophers have taken much effort to reduce *sādṛśya* to *sāmānya*. *Sādṛśya* is different from *sāmānya*; yet if there is some similarity between any two categories, then *sādṛśya* and *sāmānya* are similar. Not only this, the four realists schools of our tradition like Nyāya, Nyāya-Vaiśeṣika, Bhaṭṭa and Prābhākara admit universal or *sāmānya* as an independent existent. They also admit *upamāna.* But only the Prābhākara school admits *sādṛśya* to be a distinct kind of entity. It is quite natural to think that as all the realist schools like Nyāya, Nyāya-Vaiśeṣika, Bhāṭṭa and Prābhākara admit *sāmānya* and also *upamāna pramāṇa*, but except Prābhākara they do not admit *sādṛśya* as a distinct category, so it is better to think that there is no need to admit *sādṛśya* over and above *jāti* or *sāmānya*, especially when *sādṛśya* is reducible to *sāmānya.*

But the Prābhākaras do not admit that *sādṛśya* is reducible to *sāmānya*. Different attempts have been taken for reducing *sādṛśya* to *sāmānya*. In *Tattvacīntāmaṇi*, Gaṅgeśa himself has considered such attempts of reducing *sādṛśya* to *sāmānya*. One attempt to reduce *sādṛśya* to *sāmānya* consists in viewing *sāmānya* in the following way:

> *vijātīyatve sati avayava guṇa karma vṛtti bhūyaḥ sāmānyaṁ sādṛśyaṁ* ।

Gaṅgeśa has noted this view in page 15 of his *Upamānacintāmaṇi* (1190, vol. III). This view seems to have the support of some older school of Mīmāṁsā philosophers:

> *prācām sammatimāha* – Pragalbhācārya 1983: 4.

Second, this view is almost the same as the view which has been expressed by Kumārila in *śloka* (verse) 18 of the chapter on *upamāna* in his *Ślokavārttika*. Now let us return to the statement of *Upamānacintāmaṇi*, which is the following:

> *vijātīyatve sati avayava guṇa karma vṛtti bhūyaḥ sāmānyaṁ tat (sādṛśyaṁ).*

> A thing X will be similar to Y is X and Y are of different kinds (*vijātīya*) and if X has many (*bhūyaḥ*) universals (*sāmanya*) which are resident in the *avayavas*, *guṇa* and *karma* of Y.

The central question is: What should we understand by

(*avayava/guṇa / karma*) *sāmānya* which occurs in the quoted sentence? Should we understand *avayava sāmānya* to mean common *avayava* and *guṇa sāmānya* to mean common *guṇa*? Or should we understand by *sāmānya* the *padārtha* which is called *sāmānya*. In that case, *avayavasāmānya* should mean *avayavavṛttisāmānya*. Gaṅgeśa seems to have understood the expression in this way. We cannot understand the expression *avayavasāmānya* to mean (*sāmānya avayava*) common *avayava*. Because the *avayava*s of the two objects between which we assert similarity cannot be same; they may be only similar. But in this case there will be infinite regress. To know the things as similar, we are to know the *avayava*s to be similar. To know these *avayava*s to be similar, we need to know some other thing to be similar. And so on. So we are to assert a kind of *jāti* or *sāmānya* in the *avayava*s. Let us explain. There is similarity between an ox and a cow. Now if the similarity one explains in terms of the parts that they have, one will say that they have same kind of tail or horn, etc. (*avayava*). But to say this only is to say that they have the common property *śṛṅgatva* (property of having horn) or *lāṅgulatva* (property of having tail). And to say this only is to admit *avayava vṛtti sāmānya* (universal residing in parts). So by *sādṛśya* we are to understand *avayava vṛtti sāmānya* but not *avayava sāmānya*. Thus in this light the statement of Gaṅgeśa, i.e. *vijātīyatve sati avayava guṇa karma vṛtti bhūyaḥ sāmānya* means the following: A thing X will be similar to Y if X and Y are of different kinds (*vijātiya*) and if X has many (*bhūyaḥ*) universals (*sāmānya*) which are resident in the *avayava*s, *guṇa* and *karma* of Y.

But from this analysis it appears that *sādṛśya* or similarity can obtain between things of different kinds or *vijātīya vastu* only. But as a matter of fact there is usage as:

> *gaganaṁ gaganākaraṁ sāgaraḥ sāgaropamaḥ* |
> *rāma rāvaṇayoryuddhaṁ rāmarāvaṇayoriva* ||

In answer to this it may be said that such usages should not be taken to mean literally. So it should not be taken to mean that identically the same thing is similar to itself. This passage should be interpreted in either of the two following ways:

1. It should be taken to mean that only thing like *gagana* or battle of Rāma and Rāvaṇa has certain property.[7]

Or

2. The passage should be taken to compare one region of the sky or the ocean with another region of the sky or the ocean. Similarly one battle between Rāma and Rāvaṇa is compared with another battle between them.[8]

So from this analysis it becomes clear that either the example taken is not at all a case of similarity or if we take this as a case of similarity then the battle of Rāma and Rāvaṇa is to be taken as one battle of Rāma and Rāvaṇa with another battle of Rāma and Rāvaṇa. So whenever there is similarity the things where similarity exist must belong to two different class (*vijātīya*). That is, similarity must be there in the *vijātīya vastu* (two different class of objects).

But another objection arises against this view. If the above account is accepted, then we are to admit that similarity resides in the *vijātīya vastu*. But how can it be so? We sometimes experience a similar two lotuses which are of the same kind:

sajātye 'pi aravindadvayavat – Gaṅgeśa 1990, III: 17

Another objection is that the above account of *sādr̥śya* is in terms of many *sāmānya*, *bhūyo sāmānya*. But how manyness or multitude can be there in *sāmānya*? Again how *sādr̥śya* which is one single thing be reduced to many things or many *sāmānya*s? If *sādr̥śya* were actually many *sāmānya*s, we could not have the knowledge of *sādr̥śya* as one single thing. To this objection the following reply can be given from the side of the Bhaṭṭas or

---

[7] *gaganaṁgaganākāramityādau tu gaganādi-eva etādr̥śa dharmavat na anyaditi atra tātparyam* – Gaṅgeśa 1990, III: 43. This of course is Gaṅgeśa's reply to an objection against his own view.

[8] Cf. Ibid.

whoever wants to reduce *sādr̥śya* to *sāmānya*. It may be said that forest actually means many trees and a palace is a number of pillars and rooms, etc. Yet we experience one forest and one palace. Now what is meant by manyness or multitude of *sāmānya*? Manyness can mean different things here. Gaṅgeśa has noted three senses (1990, III: 18-19). One objection is there against taking *bhū yaḥ* in any of these senses. Many or *bhūya* (manyness) which occurs in the accounts of *sādr̥śya* in question does not mean one single thing; it means such different things as being three or four or five and so on (ibid.: 19).

Gaṅgeśa has considered here another second attempt of reducing *sādr̥śya*. This attempt is free from some of the above defects. For it is not in terms of *bhūyo* (many in quality) *sāmānya*. It is on the other hand in terms of *bahu* (many in number); and it is in terms of *dharma* (property). But *dharma* here means *sāmānya dharma*:

> *tadgata dharma iti tadgatasādhāraṇa dharma iti arthaḥ*
> – Krishnakanta 1990: 19

This second attempt to reduce *sādr̥śya* has been expressed by Gaṅgeśa thus:

> *vyāvartakadharmmāpekṣayā tadgata dharmabāhulyaṁ sādr̥śyam* ।
> – 1990, III: 19

This means a thing X is similar to another thing Y if the number of common properties (which X shares with Y) is greater in comparison to the number of uncommon properties. Uncommon properties distinguish their loci from other things. According to this account X has properties which distinguish it from Y; and also it has properties which it shares with Y. If X has greater number of *anugata* or *sādhāraṇa* (common) properties which it shares with Y than the number of properties which distinguish it from Y, then X is similar to Y. In other words X must have greater amount of agreement with Y. This greater number of agreement or the common properties is *sādr̥śya*.

The advantage of interpreting *sādṛśya* in this way is that we can explain why an elephant is not experienced as similar to a mosquito and why a *gavaya* is experienced as similar to cow. In the first case, number of uncommon properties (*vyāvartaka dharma*) is greater; in the second case the number of common properties is greater. Accordingly, it can be said that we experience similarity and speak about similarity when the number of distinguishing properties is less and common properties are same or more. In reply, Gaṅgeśa says from the Prābhākara point of view that this account is unacceptable. For we experience and use *sādṛśya* when the distinguishing properties are same but either less or more (*sadṛśa*) in number (ibid.: 20).

The third attempt to reduce *sādṛśya* has been stated by Gaṅgeśa in the sentence:

> *bhede sati tadgatabhūyaḥsāmānyavattvam sādṛśyam*
> – ibid.: 21

This can be translated in this way: when two objects are different but they have many *sāmānya*, that property of having many *sāmānya* is *sādṛśya*. This attempt is better than the previous ones. We have seen that two important features of *sādṛśya* are the following. *Sādṛśya* is *pratyāśraya bhinna,* i.e. similarity is different in each locus and it is *sapratiyogika,* it has reference to referent. But *sāmānya* differs from *sādṛśya* in these two respects. So the previous attempts to reduce *sādṛśya* could not do justice to these two features of *sādṛśya*. This third attempt of reduction is better in this respect. It is in terms of *bheda*. And *bheda* is *pratyāśrayabhinna* and *sapratiyogika*. Gaṅgeśa brings new objections here from the side of the Prābhākaras:

> *bhūyastvasāmānyapakṣoktodūṣaṇāni vihāya anyat dūṣaṇa-māha* – Pragalbhācārya 1983: 6

The Sanskrit sentence quoted above means X is similar to Y if X is other than Y and has many properties of Y:

Cf. *gobhinnatve sati gogatabahudharmavattvam* (*go*) *sādṛśyam* – ibid.: 6

This definition is in terms of *bheda* (difference) or *anyonyābhāva*. For this reason, it can do justice to the second and the fourth of the six special characteristics of *sādṛśya* we noted earlier. For *bheda* is different from one locus to the other and *bheda* is *sapratiyogika*. These two features of this new attempt to reduce *sādṛśya* to *sāmānya* makes it more attractive. But Gaṅgeśa from the side of the Prābhākaras brings new charge against it. He says in case of *bheda* we have experience and usage of the form "from that" (*tasmāt*). We say "a quality is different from a substance" (*dravyāt bhinna*). It means different from substance. But in case of *sādṛśya*, we do not say *tasmāt* or *gavayāt sadṛśa*; we do not say similar from *gavaya*. We say similar with or similar to *tena tasya vā sadṛśa* (Gaṅgeśa 1990, III: 21). Therefore we see that this attempt of reducing *sādṛśya* to *sāmānya* fails to accommodate the feature (6a) we noted in page 55 above.

Finally Gaṅgeśa, from the Prābhākara side, raises another objection. The objection is against reducing *sādṛśya* in terms of *taddharmavattva*. It means property of having the property of that (which is referred). The idea is this. Those who will not admit *sādṛśya* (similarity) as a separate category will reduce *sādṛśya*. They will reduce *sādṛśya* to *taddharmavattva*. By *tat* we are to understand that thing the similarity with which is in question. Thus when we talk about similarity with a cow (which a *gavaya* has), the cow is the *tat*. And the property of the cow is *taddharma*. But then X to be similar to Y must be different from the *tat*, i.e. Y and it must have the property of *tat*. Now the objection is that both these conditions cannot be satisfied. If a thing has *taddharma*, its *taddharmavattva* will turn it into *tat*. But if it is so, then how can it be *tat bhinna* or other than *tat*? If X has the property of Y, then it is Y and not different from Y; if it is different from Y then it cannot have the properties of Y. In Gaṅgeśa's own words:

> *taddharma-vattvam yadi sādṛśyaṁ tadā tat tadbhinnatayoḥ saṁkaraḥ syāt* –ibid.: 22

In the second place if *tatvattā* and *tattā* are the same, then even a bison (*gavaya*) could be experienced and referred to as cow (*godharmavat*) or related to that (*taddharmavat*), so it will be a cow or *tat*.

So far from the side of the Prābhākaras, Gaṅgeśa has shown that *sādṛśya* cannot be reduced. It cannot be reduced to any other category. It is irreducible. He concludes the discussion with the words *ityadhikaṁ sādṛśyam* (ibid.: 23).

II

So far we could show how Gaṅgeśa has defended the views of the Prābhākaras. Now Gaṅgeśa prepares to present the Nyāya position. He begins by saying *ucvate* (ibid.: 24). Gaṅgeśa will now defend the position of the Naiyāyikas and of the philosophers of the syncretic school. These thinkers do not admit *sādṛśya* as an additional category. Gaṅgeśa will first state a new attempt to reduce *sādṛśya* and then he will show that on this view we can explain what we could not explain by the earlier view. Gaṅgeśa will conclude his discussion of this new attempt to reduce *sādṛśya* with the word: *tasmāt na padārthāntaraṁ sādṛśyamiti* (ibid.: 45). Therefore, *sādṛśya* is not a category other than what is accepted by the syncretic school. We shall not discuss here all the points which Gaṅgeśa has discussed in pages 25 to 45 of his book. Some of the points he has discussed in this portion of the text has already been discussed by us.

There is another point to note. Krishnakanta Vidyavagisha has suggested that the view Gaṅgeśa is going to discuss now is the view of Jarat Naiyāyika (Krishnakanta 1990: 24). But the other commentators Gokulnath and Pragalbhācārya have not said any such thing. We therefore take it to be the views of some Naiyāyikas only.

Gaṅgeśa says:

asādhāraṇānya tadgatabhūyo dharmavattvam tatsādṛśyam
– 1990, III: 25

The word *asādhāraṇānya* means uncommon. Therefore *sādhāraṇa* is common. Accordingly, now the account of *sādṛśya* is this:

tadgatabhūyo sādhāraṇadharmavattvam tatsādṛśyam

It means the property of having the common character of the two where they reside. But the question is: why Gaṅgeśa has written *asādhāraṇānya,* i.e. different from *asādhāraṇa*? He could just write the *sādhāraṇa dharma*. The reason may be this. If Gaṅgeśa wrote *sādhāraṇa dharma* then even two cows would be similar. Because two cows have *sādhāraṇa dharma*s. But we generally do not say that two cows are similar. We assert similarity between such two things which do not belong to the same class. For example we assert similarity between a cow and a bison. Now the cow and the bison have their *asādhāraṇa* (extraordinary) *dharma* by which they are different. But when we assert between them *sādṛśya* and compare *go* with *gavaya,* we do that as they have some common property (also). This common property is different from their extraordinary property. As for example, a cow is different from a bison for its having the property of cowness, not of bisonness. But they are similar as they have such common properties like the property of being animal, or property of having tail or horn, etc. And these properties are *asādhāraṇānya,* i.e. *sādhāraṇa dharma* of a cow and a bison. Accordingly *sādṛśya* means "*tatgate bhūye*" *sādhāraṇadharmavattvam tatsādṛśyam*. It means a thing has similarity with another thing if it has many common properties of that other thing. Accordingly X is similar to Y means X has many common properties of Y. A bison is similar to a cow means a bison has many similar properties of a cow. But if similarity is understood in this way, then it appears that similarity is not an additional entity. It is just having many common properties with which the other thing is similar.

Gaṅgeśa says that this reduction can do justice to all the special features of *sādṛśya* noted in page 55. Moreover, this reduction avoids many defects of earlier reductions:

1. In the first place, this definition or account of *sādṛśya* is not in terms of *bheda* or *anyonyābhāva*. Therefore the objection does not arise that we would have the experience of *gavayāt sadṛśa* and not of *gavaya sadṛśa*. This objection is brought against the previous reduction.
2. The Naiyāyikas also admit that *sādṛśya* is *sapratiyogika*. It is relative or has a *pratiyogin*. What to have a *pratiyogin*? To have a *pratiyogin* does not mean that the *pratiyogin* has *avadhi* (limit). Similarly *sapratiyogika* does not mean *sāvadhika*. If Y is the *pratiyogin* of the *sādṛśya* which X has, then the *sādṛśya* (X has) is determined by (*nirūpita*) some other thing (*itara*) (ibid.: 26). Here it is Y.
3. This account of *sādṛśya* is in terms of *bahutva* (manyness). It is not in terms of *bhūyastva*. Manyness of the properties which constitute *sādṛśya* is uniformly or equally present where three or four or five common properties are there (ibid.: 26-27).
4. Against one earlier reduction, objection was raised: even a mosquito could be similar to an elephant. This objection can be brought against the present Nyāya reduction also. But Gaṅgeśa would say that it is a welcome objection. Because there are many common properties even between a mosquito and an elephant (ibid.: 27).
5. This Nyāya reduction takes note of the features (1) and 6(b) noted in page 55 above. Even when two things are otherwise dissimilar like the moon and the face, an ox and a cow, we can have close similarity (*susadṛśa*) or little similarity (*manda sadṛśa*), if there are many or less common properties.
6. Gaṅgeśa further indicates that it is quite natural to

interpret *sādṛśya* in terms of *taddharmavattva*.

If one asks a man "what is the similarity to a cow that exists in *gavaya*?", the person counts or thinks of the properties of a cow which a *gavaya* has – *taddharmavattvameva vivecayati* (ibid.: 28). In explaining Gaṅgeśa's text, Pragalbhācārya has made certain important points. We cannot discuss these points here (Pragalbhācārya 1983: 9). According to Gaṅgeśa, *sādṛśya* so far becomes *tadbhinnatvesati tadgatabhūyo* (in English translation *sādṛśya* is that which resides as many in quantity or in number in one from which the second is different. Moreover *sādṛśya* (similarity) is not other than the seven categories) or *bahudharma vattvam . . . sādṛśyam anatiriktapadārthasvarūpam*. This is exactly what Viśvanātha has later said:

> *sādṛśyam api na padārthāntaram, kintu tadbhinnatve sati tadgatabhūyodharmavattvaṁ* – 1377 (Baṅgābda): 26-27

We, therefore, can say that the definition *tadbhinnatve sati tat gatabhūya dharmavattva* can accommodate all the features of *sādṛśya*. So the definition of *sādṛśya* in terms of *tat gatabhūyo dharmavattva* is acceptable. But here the opponent may raise objection and can say that when one has the knowledge of *bhūyodharmavattva*, one does not necessarily have the knowledge of *sādṛśya*. When one has the knowledge that a bison has legs, horns, etc. one has this knowledge that a bison has many properties, i.e. *bhūyodharma*. But to have the knowledge of many properties does not imply the knowledge of *sādṛśya* (similarity). So when one has the knowledge of many properties like tail and horns in a bison, one does not necessarily have the knowledge that a bison is like a cow. So it is one thing to have the knowledge of many properties in an object and it is another thing to have the knowledge of similarity of the object with some other thing. So how can we accept that by *bhūyodharmavattva* one should understand *sādṛśya*? So when one understands that there are many properties in the X, one will understand only that X has many properties or is *bhūyodharmavān*. How will he understand that X is similar to Y? Gaṅgeśa has given answer to this question. He says when there are many properties in an object we understand that object as having many properties. But if it happens that instead of knowing those properties in that object one knows those properties in some other object, one understand that other object as similar. So when a person P knows many properties of X in Y, then P knows Y to be similar to X; he knows X and Y as similar. Take an example. One knows that properties like tailness and hornness exist in a cow (in some indirect relation). He then finds these properties in a bison. One now knows a bison as similar to a cow. So in that case the person P not only knows that there are *bhūyodharma* in a bison but he knows a bison as similar to a cow. To express this idea, Gaṅgeśa has stated:

> *anyagatabhūyodharmavattvam anyatra sādr̥śyamiti*
> – 1990, III: 34

So *sādr̥śya* is not only the possession of many properties but it is *tat bhinnatve sati tat gata bhūyodharmavattva*.

This new reduction of the Naiyāyikas is in terms of *sāmānya dharma*. Taking this to be *jāti*, a Prābhākara may raise an objection. Gaṅgeśa has noted this objection in the passage which begins *navīnāstu*. We have earlier noted that the Prābhākaras do not admit any *jāti* in things other than the substance. So in quality they will not admit any *jāti*. Here from the side of the Prābhākaras, Gaṅgeśa has taken such an example where we admit *sādr̥śya* but that cannot be explained if *sādr̥śya* is understood as a kind of *sāmānya dharma* or *jāti*. Take two different states of pleasure. Since they are just two and they are non-eternal, they cannot have a *jāti*. For when these two non-eternal things will not be there, where can that *jāti* exist? If one says that at that time *jāti* is also destroyed, then a Nāiyayika is to accept that *jāti* as destructible. So in the two qualities in question, no *jāti* or *sādhāraṇa dharma* be admitted. Yet we experience one state of pleasure as similar to another state of pleasure. Here such an experience of similarity does not depend on *sāmānya dharmavattva* (property of being manyness). Therefore the Nyāya reduction of *sādr̥śya* as *tadgatabhūyodharmavattva* cannot be accepted. It is therefore better to admit in the interest of these instances that *sādr̥śya* is an additional kind of thing. *Adhikasādr̥śyam abhyupeyam* (ibid.: 35). It means *sādr̥śya* is to be admitted as an additional *padārtha*.

Gaṅgeśa rejects this objection as insignificant. He says *tat tucchyam* (ibid.: 36). It means the former argument is absolutely insignificant. First, Gaṅgeśa says even in the two non-eternal things like two states of pleasure there can be *jāti*. The objection that the *jāti* will be destroyed when its two seats will be destroyed does not arise. For *jāti* is not destroyed due to the destruction of its locus. For a thing is destroyed if there is the cause for its destruction of its locus. For a thing is destroyed if there is the cause for its destruction, i.e. if there is *nāśaka*. Destruction of *āśraya* may be the cause for the destruction of what is by nature located (*āśrita*). Universal or *jāti* is not like that. So Gaṅgeśa says:

> *yat ca vyaktināśe jāteranityatvamāpāditam, tadapi na, nāśakābhāvāt, ata eva dvayorapi tadavasthānam.* –ibid.: 38

Gaṅgeśa also says another point. The two particular states of pleasure in question must have been caused by particular *adr̥ṣṭa* (mortal) deposition. These in their turn must have been caused due to the performance of duties. Now whoever would perform the same duties will have the same pleasure. So it cannot be said that there will be only two pleasures (ibid.: 36-37). As a result, we come to this that the view of the Prābhākaras that *sādr̥śya* is an irreducible existent is not acceptable. On the other hand, *sādr̥śya* can be said to be reducible to *sāmānya*. So the Prābhākara view is not accepted.

5

The Defence Made More Perfect
Gaṅgeśa's Lasting Contribution on Upamāna

I

In the previous chapter, I have shown the final view of Gaṅgeśa relating to *sādṛśya* (similarity). I have also shown earlier how much the notion of similarity is important in the context of *upamāna*. Now I shall consider after Gaṅgeśa the view that *upamāna* is an irreducible means of knowledge (*pramāṇa*) and this knowledge is an irreducible kind of knowledge called *upamiti*. We know that all the four realist schools of India – Prābhākaras, Bhāṭṭa Mīmāṁsakas, Naiyāyikas and the syncretic school of Nyāya-Vaiśeṣikas – admit both that *upamāna* is an irreducible *pramāṇa* and *upamiti* is an irreducible kind of knowledge. We also know that both the schools of Mīmāṁsakas admit that *upamiti* is the knowledge of *sādṛśya*. The Nyāya and the syncretic schools believe that *upamiti* or knowledge by analogy is knowledge of the relation of *śakti*. *Śakti* is the relation of meaning which a word bears to its corresponding object. Again we found that the Pābhākaras admit *sādṛśya* as an additional entity while the Bhāṭṭas do not admit *sādṛśya* as an additional entity.

Gaṅgeśa first states the view of the Bhāṭṭa Mīmāṁsakas. These Mīmāṁsakas begin in this way. Let us grant that *sādṛśya* is not an additional category. Yet the knowledge of the form that a cow (which is not being perceived at the moment) is similar to a bison (which is being perceived at the moment) is *upamiti*. This knowledge is produced when one knows from perception (*śabda*) that a bison is like a cow. Gaṅgeśa expresses this by the sentence:

mā bhūt padārthāntaraṁ tathāpi pratyakṣāt śabdāt vā gavaya go sādr̥śya jñānāt gavayasadr̥śo gauriti jñānamupamitiḥ.

– 1990, III: 45

It means *sādr̥śya* even if it is not accepted as an additional *padārtha*, yet either by perception or by testimony when one has the knowledge of the form that a bison is like a cow and then from that knows that *go* (cow) is like *gavaya* (bison) – the knowledge is *upamiti*. The Bhāṭṭas say that this knowledge cannot be a case of perception. For this knowledge is about a cow which is not present to senses of the person (knower). *Asannihitaviśeṣyakatvāt* – as the object is not in contact with sense. This knowledge cannot also be an inference. For an inference to be possible, there must be a ground (*hetu*) of inference. If one wants to infer fire in the hill, he needs smoke as the ground of inference. Similarly, one can infer that a cow is similar to a bison if one has *hetu* from which to infer. Can one infer that a cow is similar to a bison on the basis of the similarity which is there in *gavaya*? Can *gavayagata sādr̥śya* (i.e. the similarity that resides in *gavaya*) be the ground of inference? Gaṅgeśa says it is not possible. A property can be the ground of inference if it exists in *pakṣa*. When we infer "hill has fire, because of smoke" the hill is *pakṣa*, the fire is *sādhya* and the smoke is *hetu*. This smoke is there in the *pakṣa* hill. Now if one wants to infer in a cow (which is not present) the presence of similarity with a bison (*gavaya – sādr̥śya*) on the ground of *gavayagata sādr̥śya*, then this *gavayagata sādr̥śya* must be in a cow. Gaṅgeśa says this is not possible. For *gavayagata sādr̥śya* is one thing and *sādr̥śya* which is inferred (the *go gatasādr̥śya*) is another thing. Now, this *gavayagata sādr̥śya* exists in *gavaya*. It cannot exist in a cow (*go*). But if a *hetu* does not exist in a *pakṣa*, it is not a *dharma* of the *pakṣa*; if it is *apakṣa dharma* means that which resides in something other than *pakṣa*, then it is not a *liṅga* or ground of inference. So our knowledge that the cow (not present now) is similar to *gavaya* cannot be an inference from the similarity (with a cow) which is experienced in the bison. So Gaṅgeśa says:

> *nānumānam liṅgābhāvāt. na ca gavayagatam sādr̥śyam liṅgam apakṣadharmatvāt.* – ibid.: 42-43

In English translation: this piece of knowledge is not an inference as there is absence of ground (*liṅga*). The similarity that resides in a bison cannot be the ground as it does not reside in the *pakṣa* (cow) rather it resides in *gavaya* (bison) which is *apakṣa*.

An attempt has been made to show in another way that the knowledge called *upamiti* is reducible to inference. An inference of the following form can yield knowledge of similarity.

Inference One The cow (not present) is like a bison. Because, it (the cow) is *pratiyogin* (relatum) of the similarity which the bison has:

> *gavayagatasādr̥śyapratiyogitvāt gaurgavayasadr̥śa ityanumitiriti.*
>
> – ibid.: 46

The general principle is this. If anything has similarity in relation to X, then X is similar to Y. In this case *gavaya* (Y) has similarity in relation to cow (X). We experience or perceive that a bison (Y) is similar to a cow (X). The cow (X) is the *pratiyogin* (relatum) of the similarity which a bison (Y) has. So we can conclude that a cow is similar to a bison.

One may ask how we can find the above-mentioned principle of *vyāpti* (concomitant relation). We may find this relation in such two similar things which are jointly present to our senses. We may also find that this principle is illustrated in case of twins or in such cases where a brother and a sister are both present and they are very much alike. Gaṅgeśa writes:

> *atha sadr̥śadvayāntara darśane yo yadgatasādr̥śya pratiyogi sa tat sadr̥śa iti pratyakṣeṇa vyāpti grahe sati . . . gauragavayasadr̥śa ityanumitiriti.* – ibid.: 46

In English translation: when two similarities are seen in a place one that is the *pratiyogin* of the similarity is similar to it.

Gaṅgeśa rejects this attempt of the Mīmāṁsakas to reduce *upamiti* to *anumiti*. He says that one can know a bison to be similar to a cow without depending on any knowledge of *vyāpti* derived in the ways suggested above. After knowing from the utterance of some person or knowing perceptually that a bison is like a cow, one can know that a cow is like a bison.

Gaṅgeśa has another argument to reject the inference view of *upamāna*. He says that an inference cannot be constructed in the way shown above. The reason is this. In the above inference, similarity (that resides in a cow) to a bison is *sādhya* (probandum). But this was not known before. A *sādhya* is normally known before. We make fire the *sādhya* of the inference from smoke. This fire is known before when we know the *vyāpti*. Third, the ground as said before has not been perceived in the *pakṣa* (locus of inference). It may be said that in the *pakṣa go* the *liṅga* or the *gavayagatasādṛśa pratiyogitva* (relatum in relation to the similarity residing in bison) may not be perceived. It can be proved by inference. But Gaṅgeśa will say if to reduce *upamāna* to inference, we are to depend on another inference and then again on another inference, then there will be an infinite regress:

liṅgāntaragamyatvenan anavasthānāt ।

– ibid.: 47

Gaṅgeśa has noted another way of constructing the inference in which *upamāna* may be reduced.

Inference Two The (that) cow is similar to this bison. Because it has many universal properties which exist in the parts, etc. of a bison (*gavaya*). As example we can take some other bison:

gauretadgavayasadṛśaḥ gavayagatabhūyo'vayavādisāmānyavattvāt. – ibid.: 48

Gaṅgeśa rejects this reduction. He says even without knowing another bison, we can know in a cow similarity with a bison (ibid.: 47).

Gaṅgeśa next considers if *upamāna* can be reduced to *arthāpatti*. Those who will want to reduce *upamāna* to *arthāpatti* will describe the process of *upamāna* in the following way. One perceives in a bison, i.e. *gavaya go sādr̥śya* (similarity with a cow). But a bison cannot be similar to a cow if it is not similar to a bison. So one postulates (*kalpayati*) that or *tat*, i.e. *gavaya sādr̥śya* in the cow *gavi* (ibid.: 47-48).

In answer to such an attempt to reduce *upamāna* to *arthāpatti*, one may say following the Naiyāyikas that *arthāpatti* is not a separate *pramāṇa*. It is one type of *anumāna* called *vyatireki anumāna*. We can construct an argument here. Those who want to reduce *upamāna* to some other *pramāṇa* would say, either *sādr̥śya* in the cow (not present) is known *arthāpatti* or it is known through *vyatireki anumāna*. In either case, there is no need to admit a separate *pramāṇa* called *upamāna*. Second, if for knowledge of similarity a separate *pramāṇa* like *upamāna* is needed, then for the knowledge of *vaidharmya* (dissimilarity) also we would require still another *pramāṇa*:

> *gāvi karabha vaidharmyajñānamapi mānāntarāt syāt iti.*
>
> – ibid.: 49

Gaṅgeśa says in reply that *vaidharmya* can be known either through *anupalabdhi* (cf. ibid.: 49) or through *pratyakṣa*. It all depends on what is to be understood by *vaidharmya* or what it is to know that X is dissimilar to Y. It may mean knowing in the cow is the absence of the property of the camel (*karabha*); or it may mean our knowing in the cow is such property which does not exist in the *karabha* (*karabhāvr̥ttidharmavattvam*). Gaṅgeśa has discussed many more points before he concludes the discussion of Mīmāṁsā account of *upamāna* with the words *vigarhitametat* (ibid.: 54). It means the Mīmāṁsā view is unacceptable. This remark shows that Gaṅgeśa considers the Mīmāṁsā view as thoroughly unacceptable. It cannot be accepted that the similarity in the cow (not present now) is not known in any other way; and that is why a separate *pramāṇa* called *upamāna* is needed.

II

In the previous section it has been stated from the side of the old Naiyayikas that the Mīmāṁsā view is objectionable (*vigarhitam etat iti* – ibid.: 54). For *upamiti* means the knowledge that the thing not being perceived at the moment (the cow in the town) is similar to the thing being perceived now (e.g. *gavaya*). This similarity is a different similarity. This is not the similarity which the perceived bison has. The knowledge of *vyāpti* gives us the knowledge of similarity in a cow. A knowledge so based on *vyāpti* is (*vyātirekī*) an inference according to the Naiyāyikas and *arthāpatti* according to the Mīmāṁsakas (ibid.: 55). In either case, knowledge of *sādṛśya* is not a distinct type of knowledge called *upamiti*. And as a result *upamāna* as understood by the Mīmāṁsakas is not an irreducible (*svatantra*) *pramāṇa*.

After presenting the Jarannaiyāyika (the old Nyāya) view of *upamāna*, Gaṅgeśa now tells us how such a Naiyāyika defends his own position. The position of a Jarannaiyāyika is that the *upamiti* or the result of *upamāna pramāṇa* (*upamāna phalam*) is the knowledge of the form "this is the referent of the word *gavaya*":

> *ayam gavaya śabdavācya iti matirupamāna phalam.*
>
> – ibid.: 56

Following are the reasons why knowledge of this type is said to be the result of irreducible means of knowledge called *upamāna*. So far as the Naiyāyikas are concerned every knowledge must come from either *pratyakṣa* or *anumāna* or *śabda*, if it is not the result of *upamāna*. Now the knowledge in question cannot come from some linguistic utterance alone (*atideśavākya*): *na ceyaṁ vākya mātrāt* (ibid.: 56). It means this is not only from the sentence. Let us consider a standard case of what a Naiyāyika takes to be a case of *upamāna*. A person P_1 lives in a town. He has seen many cows. He has never gone to the forest and has never seen the animal called *gavaya*. He has heard the word *gavaya* but does not know what this word means or refers to. He asks a forester, who is in a position to know "what like is a *gavaya*" (*kidṛśa gavaya iti jijñāsā* . . . – ibid.: 56)? Now the forester makes the linguistic utterance "*gavaya* is like a cow". Can this linguistic utterance (*vākya*) alone give the knowledge called *upamiti*? If it could, then P_1 could know the meaning of the word *gavaya* without ever seeing an instance of *gavaya* (*apratyakṣīkṛtapiṇḍasyāpi prasaṅgāt*. – ibid.: 56). But as a matter of fact P_1 does not know what a *gavaya* is or he cannot have the knowledge of the form *ayam gavaya padavācyaḥ* (this is the meaning of the word *gavaya*) till he goes to the forest and sees the actual *gavaya*. Therefore to have the sort of knowledge in question one must depend on perception. But perception also cannot be the sufficient condition of this knowledge. For if a person was not told that *gavaya* was like a cow, he would not have the type of knowledge in question even if a *gavaya* were before his eyes. It therefore follows that none of the two – statement of analogy (*atideśa vākya*) and perception of similarity (*sādṛśya pratyakṣa*) – is a sufficient condition though each of them is a necessary condition. Gaṅgeśa considered a third possibility. The type of knowledge in question is the result of the combination (*samāhāra*) of the two. After a long discussion Gaṅgeśa rejected this alternative (ibid.: 57f.).

Upamiti is partially caused by *pratyakṣa*. But this does not make *upamiti pratyakṣa*. Because even in the production of *anumiti* and *śabda*, *pratyakṣa* makes some contribution; *pratyakṣa* can be said to be *prayojaka* (a condition) of *anumiti* and *śabda*. But still these are not included or reduced into *pratyakṣa*. Nor can we say that the result of the *vākya* and *pratyakṣa* combined is not knowledge proper. If thus there results a knowledge proper from *vākya* and *pratyakṣa* along with memory, then that is a distinct kind of knowledge called *upamiti*. This is the view of old Naiyāyika like Jayanta Bhaṭṭa:

> *tasmāt āgama pratyakṣābhyāmanyat evasmr̥tisahitaṁ sādr̥śya jñānam upamāna pramāṇaṁ iti jarannaiyāyikā jayanta prabhitayoḥ.* – ibid.: 61

Gaṅgeśa does not accept the view of *upamāna* of the Naiyāyikas of earlier days. But the point of criticism he brings does not seem to be very convincing. I have discussed this in my previous book (Uma Chattopadhyay 2009). Gaṅgeśa says that a south Indian may have the knowledge of the form "this is *karabha* (camel)". This knowledge is based on dissimilarity with every known animal familiar in the south. Now Gaṅgeśa argues that according to the old Naiyāyikas this cannot be knowledge by analogy. For here there is no similarity (*na tāvat upamānam, sādr̥śyabhāvāt* – Gaṅgeśa 1990, III: 62) or knowledge of similarity. This rather is a case of knowledge by disanalogy or dissimilarity. Is it then a separate type of knowledge, different from perception, inference and even knowledge by analogy? Gaṅgeśa says that is not possible: *na ca pramāṇantaram sambhavati* (ibid.: 62). It means there is no possibility of *pramāṇa* other than the accepted *pramāṇa*. What he means is that the conditions for any other kind of knowledge (*pramāṇantara*) do not obtain. The implication therefore is that the knowledge that "this is *karabha*" is to be included within the kind of knowledge called *upamiti*. But the theory of analogy (*upamāna*) as has been developed by the Naiyāyikas of earlier days does not have room for the knowledge of *śakti* which results from the knowledge of dissimilarity. Gaṅgeśa therefore offers his own account of knowledge by analogy and he begins with the word *ucyate* (ibid.: 62). And he concludes this statement with the word *paramārthataḥ* (ibid.: 66).

In the first place, Gaṅgeśa says that we cannot learn the meaning of words like *gavaya* without involving reference to some property which is common to (or which is exclusive common property of) all the individual *gavaya*s (ibid.: 62-63). In standard cases, this property should be *śakyatāvacchedaka*.[1] Where *śakyatāvacchedaka* property is not available, *upalakṣaṇa* (an incidental characteristic) must be available. In the next place, he shows that we cannot learn the meaning of the word like *gavaya* in the way in which we learn the meaning of such words as (1) *caitra*, (2) *dik* or *ākāśa*, (3) *pācaka*, (4) *svarga*. He says that the word *gavaya* is more like the word *pṛthivī*. The word *pṛthivī* refers to all and only what has *pṛthivītva* and what has also as *upalakṣaṇa gandha* (smell). Similarly, the word *gavaya* refers to all and only the things which have *gavayatva* and which also have similarity with a cow as *upalakṣaṇa*. Pragalbhācārya understands the position of Gaṅgeśa stated in the passage mentioned above in the following way. Among the five types of denoting words, name or *saṁjñā* (Udayanācārya 1967: 363), the word *gavaya* which is like the word *pṛthivī* belongs to the type *naimittikī saṁjñā*. So both the words *pṛthivī* and *gavaya* are *naimittikī saṁjñā*. Now the words which are *naimittikī saṁjñā* have associated with them some universal as *nimitta* or *pravṛtti-nimitta*. Such *nimitta* acts as the criterion of the correct application of the word. In case of the word *gavaya*, the *nimitta* is *gavayatva*. In the case of the word *pṛthivī*, the *nimitta* is *pṛthivītva*. Pragalbhācārya further clarifies the point of Gaṅgeśa. The word *gavaya* is thus related by the relation of *śakti* to the thing which has *gavayatva*. Otherwise we could not admit a *pramāṇa* called *upamāna* (Pragalbhācārya 1983: 30). The idea seems to be the following. Linguistic utterance (*atideśa vākya*) like "*gavaya* is like a cow" helps us to have the knowledge that the word *gavaya* refers to *gavaya*. But the word *gavaya* refers to all the individual *gavaya*s not individually but as members of the class *gavaya*. So

---

[1] *Śakya* means the word referred *avacchedaka* means the characterizer, accordingly *śakyatāvacchedaka* means characterizer of the word referred.

our knowledge of *śakti* or denotative meaning takes the form "the things that have *gavayatva* (*gavayatva viśiṣṭa*) are denoted by the word *gavaya* (*gavaya padavācya*)". This knowledge, *gavayatva viśiṣṭa gavaya padavācya*, or the *upamiti* cannot result directly or only from the linguistic utterance or the statement of analogy (*atideśa vākya*). For the statement of analogy does not tell us what has *gavayatva* is the denotation of the word *gavaya*. It tells on the other hand that *gavaya* is what is similar to a cow. Now *gavayatva* is the property which characterizes *gavaya*s when we know them as the referent of the word *gavaya*. So *gavayatva* is the *śakyatāvacchedaka* so far as the word *gavaya* is concerned. The property "similarity with cow" which characterizes *gavaya*s in the statement of analogy is the *upalakṣaṇa*. Thus when we know the meaning of the word *gavaya*, we actually know that the *gavaya*s which have *go-sādṛśya* as *upalakṣaṇa* and *gavayatva* as *śakyatāvacchedaka* are the meaning of the word *gavaya*,

> *sādṛśyadi upalakṣite gavayatvādau gavayādipadānām śaktiriti tu paramārthataḥ.* – Gaṅgeśa 1990, III: 65- 66

To translate: words like *gavaya*, etc. which are characterized by such incidental properties like similarity, etc., mean the animal bison (*gavaya*), etc. This *śakti* of the word *gavaya*, etc. cannot be known without *upamiti*. If knowledge of these words were known by other means, then *gavayatva*, etc. would not be *śakyatāvacchedaka*. And if *gavayatva* were not *śakyatāvacchedaka*, then *upamiti* as formulated above would not be a case of *pramā*. It would be a false belief. But in that case *upamāna* also would not be a *pramāṇa*.

The opponent may ask now: Can one have the knowledge after hearing the statement of analogy that *gosādṛśya upalakṣita gavayatva viśiṣta gavaya padavācya*? For there is nothing in the statement of analogy to recall (*upasthita*) *gavayatva*. *Na ca pūrvam gavayatvaṁ upasthitaṁ, upasthāpakābhāvāt* (ibid.: 66). The opponent further says that Gaṅgeśa will land himself in circularity if he says that the word *gavaya* (in the statement of analogy) itself recalls *gavayatva*. For the word cannot recall the *gavayatva* unless we know the meaning of it, and we do not know the meaning of it unless we know *gavayatva viśiṣṭa* is *gavaya padavācya*. Some may say that what we know from *upamāna* is the following: "This is that cow-like-thing which we learnt (from the statement of analogy) as the referent of the word *gavaya*" (cf. ibid.). Gaṅgeśa cannot however accept this.

The important point in Gaṅgeśa's theory of *upamiti* is that *gavayatva* and not similarity (*sādṛśya*) is held to be the *śakyatāvacchedaka* or *pravṛtti-nimitta*. *Na hi sādṛśyam eva nimittam* (ibid.: 67). Gaṅgeśa has offered two arguments why *sādṛśya* cannot be the *nimitta*, i.e. the *pravṛtti-nimitta* or *śakyatāvacchedaka* in respect of the word *gavaya*. The conclusion that *sādṛśya* is not *nimitta* or not the (necessary) criterion for the use of the word *gavaya* (*śakyatāvacchedaka*) was told before even by Udayanācārya (*sādṛśyasyānimittatvāt* – 1962: 3.11). Gaṅgeśa's first argument is this. If similarity with cow were the necessary criterion, then one who has not experienced this similarity and cannot use the word *gavaya*: *apratītānām avyavahāra prasaṅgāt* (Gaṅgeśa 1990, III: 67). To translate: the person who does not know will not be able to use.

The point of the argument has been more clearly brought out by Pragalbhācārya. Pragalbhācārya says that if similarity with the cow is the necessary criterion for the use of the word *gavaya*, then a forester who has not seen a cow cannot use the word *gavaya*. But he does correctly make use of the word *gavaya*. This shows that one need not experience cow similarity in an animal in order to apply the word *gavaya* to it (Pragalbhācārya 1983: 20). This is the first argument of Gaṅgeśa against the view that similarity is the necessary criterion (*pravṛtti-nimitta*) for the use of the words. But Gaṅgeśa's second argument against the view that similarity is the criterion is more fundamental. This is the argument from *gaurava* or violation of the law of parsimony. Pragalbhācārya says: *mūla doṣam āha gauravāt ca iti* (ibid.). The point is this. In comparison to the unanalysable universal *gavayatva* the property "cow similarity" is complex. And a criterion in terms of a simple property should be preferred to another in terms of a complex property. The maxim is, if a simpler property (*laghu dharma*) can be found as determinant or *avacchedaka* (say *avacchedaka* of *śakyatā*), then a complex property should not be admitted as *avacchedaka*. *Sambhavati ca laghau dharma gurau tadabhāvāt.*[2]

It may be granted on the grounds stated above that cow similarity (*go sādr̥śya*) is not the criterion. But *gavayatva* was not known or presented before. *Nāpi gavayatvaṁ tadanupasthiteḥ* (Gaṅgeśa 1990, III: 67).

Some may argue that from the *atideśa vākya* itself we may know *gavayatva viśiṣṭa gavaya* is the referent of the word *gavaya*. The process is the following. One first hears the *atideśa vākya* (statement of analogy). One knows from it that things similar to a cow is the referent of the word *gavaya*. Then one comes to doubt and enquire whether cow-similarity is the *upalakṣaṇa* or *nimitta* (*śakyatāvacchedaka*). Consideration of the fact that cow similarity is more complex convinces one that cow similarity cannot be the *nimitta*. Finally, he comes to interpret the statement of analogy. Ordinarily, apparently and explicitly the statement means "the thing which has cow-similarity is the referent of the word *gavaya*". But he interprets it to mean "things having *gavayatva* are the referent of the word *gavaya* (*gavayatva viśiṣṭa gavaya padavācya*)". Or he interprets it thus – *go sādr̥śya upalakṣita gavayatva viśiṣṭa* (*prāṇī*) *gavaya padavācya*. The way the statement of analogy "*gavaya* is like cow" is interpreted to mean *go sādr̥śya upalakṣita gavayatva viśiṣṭa* (*prāṇī*) *gavaya padavācya* is comparable to the way the statement *gaṅgāyām ghoṣaḥ* is understood to mean

---

2 This is, however, generally true but not universally as has been pointed out by Raghunatha Siromani in his *Avacchedakatvaniryukti* (1968: 1).

the village of the Ghoṣa's is on the *bank* of the river, the Ganges (ibid.: 68-69).

Gaṅgeśa rejects this line of reasoning. His arguments are the following. He says that the statement of analogy cannot be compared with the statement *gaṅgāyām ghoṣaḥ*. For in the latter case the things *gaṅgā* (or the flow of water) and the village (or the place of living) cannot be combined to make a coherent sense. For what can it mean if one says "a village of men is *in* the flowing water? This allows us to (re)interpret it in the way shown above":

> *gaṅgāyām ghoṣaḥityatra tu padārtha eva anvaya ayogya iti yuktam tatra mānāntarāpekṣaṇam* – ibid.: 70

But the sentence *go sadṛśa gavaya* makes perfect sense. It means "what has similarity with a cow is (has the property of being) called by the word *gavaya*". So here we have no reason to involve *gavayatva* (i.e. interpret *go sādṛśya* as *gavayatva*). Therefore *gavayatva* (as *pravṛtti-nimitta*) be known by some source other than the statement of analogy itself (ibid.: 69). Still it may be said that re-interpretation is necessary. For if the *atideśa vākya* is taken in the straightforward sense, the intention of the speaker will not be clear. The intention (*tātparya*) is not just to say "what is cow-like is *gavaya*". The intention is what has *gavayatva* is called *gavaya*. It may be said in reply that we cannot take a whole sentence in some extended sense. For extended sense (*lakṣaṇā*) is possible only in case of individual words within a sentence (*pada lakṣaṇā*) but not in case of a sentence as a whole; *vākye na lakṣaṇā* (ibid.: 71).

Our purpose will not be served if we here take only the word *go sadṛśa* in its extended sense (*lakṣaṇā*) to mean *gavayatva*. For if we take the expression *go-sadṛśa*, which occurs in the statement of analogy, in the extended sense to mean *gavayatva* then we can get the following information from the statement of analogy. We get the information that *gavayatva* which is called *gavaya*. Let us explain. The statement of analogy is *go sadṛśa gavaya* (*gavaya* is similar to a cow). We know from the context what is being said: *go sadṛśa gavaya padavācyaḥ* (what is similar to a cow is called *gavaya*). Now the expression *go sadṛśa* is taken in the extended sense of *gavayatva*. Accordingly, the statement of analogy that comes to mean *gavayatva* is *gavaya padavācyaḥ* (*gavayatva* is called *gavaya*). But we know that *upamiti* is the knowledge of the individual which has *gavayatva*; it is not the knowledge of *gavayatva* (*vyakti vācyatā na jñāyeta tat śabdāt* – ibid.: 72). In other words *upamiti* is the knowledge "the individual animal which has *gavayatva* and is called *gavaya*"; it is not merely "*gavayatva* which is called *gavaya*". So *lakṣaṇā* will not help us to have the knowledge of individual as qualified by the universal property to be the referent of the name. Gaṅgeśa therefore says we must (*avaśya*) admit (*svīkaraṇīyam*) a separate means of knowledge (*mānāntara*), i.e. *upamāna*, as knowing (*grāhaka*) that a qualified individual (here qualified by *viśiṣṭa* the universal property *gavayatva*) is called *gavaya* (*viśiṣṭa vācyatāgrāhakamānāntaram avaśyaṁ svīkaraṇīyam* (ibid.: 72). It may be said in reply that since the word *go sadṛśa* signifies (through *lakṣaṇā*) *gavayatva* and *gavayatva* is the *dharma* of *gavaya*, the word signifies (the individual) *gavaya* also. Because it is said *yanniṣṭha dharma yatpadavācyaḥ sa api tatvācya iti niyamaḥ* (ibid.: 71). But this cannot be said because there is counter example to the rule. A *jāti pada* "*gotva*" does not signify the *vyakti* which has *jāti* (ibid.: 72). It is not denied, however, that a word which signifies an individual cow also signifies the universal cowness.

For different reasons it cannot be said that the intention of the speaker settles the matter. What is the intention behind the utterance of the statement of analogy? It is to intimate that the individual *gavaya* is the referent of the word *gavaya* and so through *lakṣaṇā* which preserves intention we know that the animal which has *gavayatva* (the *pravṛttinimitta*) is the denotation of the word *gavaya* (ibid.: 72-73). It should be noted that *lakṣaṇā* is admitted primarily to preserve speaker's intention and determine meaning accordingly.

It is already known that the elites (*śiṣṭa*) use the expression *gavaya*, so it must have a referent. In consideration of parsimony, we decide that the referent of the word *gavaya* is what has *gavayatva* and not what has cow similarity. Now parsimony is not a *pramāṇa*. It can be an additional support to an existing *pramāṇa*. So there must be some *pramāṇa* to yield this knowledge (that *gavayatvaviśiṣṭaprāṇī gavayapadavācyaḥ*) with the consideration of parsimony as its aid or *sahakārī* (cf. ibid.: 74-75). And this *pramāṇa* is *upamāna*. Now those who do not admit *upamāna* as a separate *pramāṇa* may say that the *pramāṇa* in question (which in this case is assisted by consideration of parsimony) is *anumāna* (*atha astu anumānam* – ibid.: 75). If this is true, then knowledge of *śakti* or the alleged knowledge called *upamiti* is produced by inference. Thus *upamāna* is reduced to inference. The form of the inference is what we find in Vācaspati Miśra (1985: 171) and Vallabhācārya (1934: 531). The inference is of the following form:

> *gavaya śabdo gavayatva viśiṣṭa dharmī vācakaḥ asati vṛtyantare vṛddhai prayujyamānatvāt govi go śabdavat iti.*
>
> – Gaṅgeśa 1990, III: 75

> The word *gavaya* denotes the thing which has the property *gavayatva*; because experts or those who know, use it to denote this object and the word does not denote any other thing; example is the word cow which denotes what has cowness.

Gaṅgeśa says in reply that we may grant this inference can give us the knowledge that the word *gavaya* is the name of the individual animal which has *gavayatva*. But we cannot know from this inference that *gavayatva* is the *pravṛtti-nimitta*. *Gavayatva* coexists in *gavaya* with the property (*gavaya-pada*) *vācyatva* or *śakyatva*; yet from such coexistence (*sāmānādhikaraṇya*), we cannot conclude that *gavayatva* is the *śakyatā* (or *vācyatā*) *avacchedaka*. For such *sāmānādhikaraṇya* obtains between cow-similarity and *gavaya-pada-vācyatā*. But *go sādr̥śya* is only *upalakṣaṇa* and not (*vācyatā-*) *avacchedaka*.

Now the opponent can say that on the ground of *lāghavagaurava tarka* we can exclude cow-similarity. And there will remain only *gavayatva* as *pravr̥tti nimitta* or *śakyatāvacchedaka*. We can formulate the point in this way:

> The word *gavaya* has associated with it the property *gavayatva* as *pravr̥tti nimitta*. Because while this word has some *pravr̥tti nimitta* associated with it, it has no property other than *gavayatva* so associated with it, which does not have the one, does not have the other. – ibid.: 76-77

It may be noted that we have formulated the point as *vyatirekī anumāna*. But how can *tarka* help this *vyatirekī anumāna*? *Tarka* in question here is *lāghava/gaurava tarka*. And this *tarka* has to do with apprehension of *vyāpti*. In answer, it may be said that *tarka* seems to play some role here. Instead of first postulating a new *pramāṇa* and holding *tarka* to be an aid of that, it is better and reasonable to take *tarka* to be an accessory of a known *pramāṇa* (ibid.: 79-80). Accordingly, it is better to conclude that first *sāmānyataḥ dr̥ṣṭa anumāna* and *tarka* together show that the word *gavaya* does not denote any other thing. Later *vyatirekī anumāna* shows that the word has the property *gavayatva* associated with it as *pravr̥tti nimitta*.

III

Now let us reconstruct and summarize the argument in our own way. A person knows the word *gavaya* but does not know to which thing this word applies or which thing the word denotes. He is told "*gavaya* is like a cow". Later on he comes to have the knowledge that the word *gavaya* denotes an animal which has both *gavayatva* and similarity with a cow. He could not have derived this knowledge from the statement of analogy quoted above. For neither directly nor through *lakṣaṇā* can the sentence "*gavaya* is like a cow" give this knowledge. The word *gavaya*, contained in the sentence "*gavaya* is like a cow", cannot also give this knowledge through *lakṣaṇā*. Even so we cannot say that knowledge is derived from *upamāna* as an additional *pramāṇa*. For it can be derived either from the statement of analogy and *tarka* or from inference and *tarka*. *Tarka* is the aid (*sahakārī*). Here *tarka* consists in the consideration of logical economy (*lāghava*)[3] or the violation of it *gaurava*.

Now the central question, whether *upamāna* is an additional *pramāṇa* or not, may be resolved in this way. It is still debatable whether there is such a *pramāṇa* called *upamāna* or not. The procedure generally accepted as justified is, not to postulate a new entity or item (here *pramāṇa*) unless it is absolutely necessary. So the common practice is to try to explain a given phenomenon in terms of what has already been accepted or about which there is no controversy. In the situation in question, there is no doubt about two things. First, *śabda* (linguistic utterance or statement of analogy) plays an important role in the production of knowledge by analogy. Second, *anumāna* (inference) is a *pramāṇa* or source of knowledge. So every effort should be made to show that the knowledge in question which the Naiyāyikas describe as *upamiti* comes from *śabda* or inference. On behalf of the opponents, Gaṅgeśa elaborately describes such efforts. In other words, he shows in detail how the knowledge of the form "the thing which has *gavayatva* is the referent of the word *gavaya*" may be explained by those who do not admit *upamāna* to be a separate *pramāṇa*.

The Naiyāyikas from the ancient time are convinced that the type of knowledge in question cannot be derived from any source of knowledge other than *upamāna*. Vātsyāyana raised and answered the question "what does *upamāna* do in such cases" (cf. Chapter 1 and see Vātsyāyana 1967: 355). Udayanācārya had also said in clear terms that the knowledge called *upamiti*

---

3 Prof. Gopinath Bhattacharya in his edition of *Tarkasaṁgraha* translated *lāghava* as logical economy (cf. Gopinath Bhattacharya, 1976: 223).

cannot be derived either from *anumāna* or from *śabda*.[4] Now here the statement of analogy cannot yield the knowledge that the individual thing or animal which has (the universal) property *gavayatva* is the meaning or referent of the word *gavaya*. In the literal sense of it, the sentence tells us that the word *gavaya* refers to what has cow-similarity. But if a word refers to a thing because it has a particular property then that property, becomes *śakyatāvacchedaka*.

Now if the *atideśa vākya* is understood literally and if it is taken as the source of our knowledge of *śakti*, then in the case cow-similarity should be admitted to be the *śakyatāvacchedaka* in respect of the word *gavaya*. But the difficulty in that case will be the following. A cow can also become *gavaya* or the denotation of the word *gavaya*. For any single cow has cow-similarity (similarity to some other cow). This was already pointed out by the *prācīna* Naiyāyikas (Uma Chattopadhyay 2009: 137). The *navya* Naiyāyikas further add that compared to the property *gavayatva*, the property *go-sādṛśya* is more complex. A more complex property cannot be *avacchedaka*. How can then *atideśa vākya* tell us that *gavayatva* is *pravṛtti nimitta* or *śakyatāvacchedaka*? The sentence can do this if it can yield the knowledge that the thing which has *gavayatva* is a referent of the word *gavaya*. But for this we are to take either the whole sentence or the word *go sadṛśa* contained in it, in the secondary and extended sense (*lakṣaṇā*). The conditions under which we can take an expression in the extended sense do not hold here. But there is another way which may be called *tarka*. *Tarka* is not a source of knowledge (*pramāṇa*):

> *tarko na pramāṇasaṁgṛhīto, na pramāṇāntaraṁ, pramāṇānām anugrāhakaḥ tattvajñānāya kalpate.* – Vātsyāyana 1985: 53

---

4 We shall see later that it is not the view of the Naiyāyikas that the knowledge of *śakti* cannot be derived from any source other than *upamāna*. But in certain situation, as in *go-gavaya* case under reference, the knowledge is derived from *upamāna* and from no other source.

But it is a type of consideration which renders some help to *pramāṇa*; with the help of *tarka* a *pramāṇa* can do its job more easily and efficiently. There are different types of *tarka*. One type of *tarka* consists in a sort of consideration which enables us (of course through *pramāṇa*) to ascertain relation of *vyāpti*. Roughly speaking this sort of *tarka* is called *vyāpti-grāhaka-tarka*. A second type of *tarka* is there; it is a sort of eliminative consideration. The *tarka* which takes into consideration the question of relative complexity (*gaurava*) and simplicity (*lāghava*) is of this second type. With the help of this sort of *tarka*, the *atideśa vākya* can tell us that the thing having *gavayatva* is the referent of the word *gavaya*. For though ordinarily this sentence says that the thing having cow-similarity is the referent of the word *gavaya*, *lāghava tarka* rejects the claim of cow-similarity to be *pravṛtti nimitta* here. So we come to realize here that *pravṛtti nimitta* is *gavayatva*. It is in this way that the *śabda* (*atideśa vākya*) can be said to yield the knowledge which the Naiyāyikas called *upamāna*.

In short, we are first convinced that the word *gavaya* must have some referent; for it is used by persons who are knowledgeable and *śiṣṭa*. Then with the help of considerations of logical economy (*lāghavāt*), we decide that the thing (animal) which has *gavayatva* is the referent in question. But this sort of consideration or *tarka* is not by itself a source of knowledge or *pramāṇa*. It is rather an aid to some *pramāṇa*. It is *pramāṇa sahakārī* in the words of Gaṅgeśa (1990, III: 74). If the *pramāṇa sahakārī tarka* is there then there must be that *pramāṇa* of which this *tarka* is *sahakārī*:

> *ato yat pramāṇa sahakārī tat pramāṇāntaram āstheyam.*
>
> – ibid.: 75

The opponents would hold that this *pramāṇa* is *śabda* or *anumāna* (Udayanācārya 1941: 198, 200). In other words, *anumāna* or *śabda*, which is already admitted to be a *pramāṇa* may give us knowledge of the meaning relation with the help of *tarka*. If this be the case, then no scope is there for postulating a new and additional *pramāṇa* called *upamāna*; nor is there any scope to hold that *tarka* in question acts as an aid of this new *pramāṇa*:

> *na tu mānāntaraṁ kalpayitvā tarkaḥ sahakārī kalpyate.*
> – Gaṅgeśa 1990, III: 77

In reply to such an argument the following may be said. We may generally know or can infer in a general way (*sāmānyatodṛṣṭa*) that this word (*gavaya*) has some property associated with it which is the criterion for the correct application of the word (*idam sapravṛtti-nimittakaṁ* – ibid.: 77). From *tarka* (eliminative consideration), we may know that no other property is (associated as) *pravṛtti nimitta* (*anyancca na pravṛttinimittamiti* – ibid.: 77). But how do we know that the word *gavaya* has *gavayatva* as *pravṛtti nimitta*? Without the help of some other *pramāṇa* we cannot know it:

> *gavayatva pravṛtti-nimittakaṁ gavaya padaṁ iti mānāntaraṁ vinā apratīteḥ.* – ibid.: 78

And *upamāna* is this new *pramāṇa*.

There is a difference between taking *tarka* as *sahakārī* of *anumāna* (such as *sāmānyato-dṛṣṭa-anumāna*) and taking *tarka* as *sahakārī* of *upamāna*. In the first case, one admits *tarka* to be *sahakārī* of a *pramāṇa* which is already admitted to be there. But in the second case, one must first postulate a new *pramāṇa*, that is to say, *upamāna* and then further postulate that *tarka* is the *sahakārī* of it. It is always better and economical (*laghu*) to postulate one thing rather than two things. And so it is better to hold that the meaning relation, of the word *gavaya* to the thing which has *gavayatva*, is known through *anumāna* assisted by *tarka*.

We have already considered an argument which shows that *anumāna* with the help of *tarka* cannot produce the knowledge of *śakti*. Another argument shows that the statement of analogy cannot be said to give us the knowledge of *vyāpti*:

na ca vyāpti paraṁ idaṁ vākyam . . . iti vācyaṁ – ibid.: 81

Let us explain. Consider the situation under which the statement of analogy has been uttered or could be uttered. If someone first knew what is similar to cow (*go sadr̥śa*), then he could ask of which word is this the referent (*sa kim śabda vācya*). In answer to this question the statement of analogy might be uttered. If the situation were like this, then we could say that the statement of analogy produced the knowledge of *vyāpti* of the form what is similar to cow is the referent of the word *gavaya*. And then we could have the inference of the form "this is the referent of the word *gavaya* because it has similarity with cow. As for example the particular thing or animal which was known at the time of hearing *atideśa vākya*."

ayam gavaya padavācyaḥ gosadr̥śavāt atideśa-kālāvagata piṇḍavat iti. – ibid.: 81

There are two objections against the above attempt to show that our knowledge of the meaning of the word *gavaya* is derived from inference. The first objection has been briefly stated by Pragalbhācārya. It has not been mentioned by Gaṅgeśa. Pragalbhācārya says that even if the situation were conceived in the way the opponent did it, the right sort of knowledge of meaning relation cannot be derived from *anumāna*. The statement of analogy gives us the knowledge of *vyāpti*, according to the opponents, if we understand the situation of its utterance. On the basis of that *vyāpti* we can have the following inference:

ayam gavaya padavācyaḥ, go sadr̥śavāt, atideśa kālāvagata piṇḍavat iti. – ibid.

This (animal) is the referent of the word *gavaya* because it has similarity with cow, e.g. the particular animal known at the time of hearing the statement of analogy.

As the opponents understand the situation, the *vyāpti* involved here is this: whatever "has similarity to cow" is referent of the word *gavaya*. Now Pragalbhācārya points out that from this inference we cannot know that the animal having *gavayatva* as *pravr̥tti-nimitta* is the referent of the word *gavaya*:

> *gavayatvena pravr̥tti-nimittena 'gavaya pada vācyaḥayam' iti rūpam jñānam na ukta anumānāt siddhati.*
>
> – Pragalbhācārya 1983: 26

But it is this type of knowledge which we get from *upamāna*. Therefore the first objection against the opponent is that he has failed to show that *anumāna* can do the job of *upamāna*.

As we have said before, this first objection has not been discussed by Gaṅgeśa. Gaṅgeśa points out a different defect. He points out that the opponent read or understood the situation wrongly. The case is not that the city dweller first knew certain animal as similar to cow. And then he asked the question "of which word is that animal (which is similar to cow) the referent?" If the situation were like this then the forester could tell the city dweller *gavaya śabda vācyaḥ* (*ayam*) or (that animal) is the referent of the word *gavaya*. And then the city dweller could derive from the utterance of the forester a knowledge of the *vyāpti* of the form "what is similar to cow is the referent of the word *gavaya*". Actually, however, the city dweller asked a different question. He asked "what the animal named by the word *gavaya* is like?

> *kintu sāmānyat gavaya padārthaṁ avagatya 'sa kīdr̥giti'.*
>
> – Gaṅgeśa 1990, III: 81-82

Also

> *kintu 'gavaya śabda vācyaḥkīdr̥g iti pr̥ṣṭaṁ.*
>
> – Pragalbhācārya 1983: 26

The right answer to this question on the part of the forester must be formulated in the sentence *yo gavaya śabda vācyaḥ sa go sadr̥śa*, (what is the referent of the word *gavaya* is similar to cow). If this sentence is taken to state the relation of *vyāpti*, then that relation must be the relation between *gavaya pada vācyatva* and *go-sādṛśya*. In other words, whatever is the referent of the word *gavaya* is similar to cow. From this, it is clear that *gavaya pada vācyatva* is the *vyāpya* of the ground of inference. But similarity to cow is not the *vyāpya*. But the opponent used similarity to cow as the ground of the inference which he constructed.

We have considered the situation in which one asks the question to which the statement of analogy is an answer. But what is the import of the question raised in such situation by persons like the city dweller in our example? Does the inquirer want to know the definition which enables one to make right application of a word? Gaṅgeśa rejects this suggestion, viz.:

> *lakṣaṇa param idam vākyam kim lakṣako asau iti praśnārthaḥ.*
>
> – Gaṅgeśa 1990, III: 82

Gaṅgeśa would rather hold that the city dweller intended to ask "what was the *pravṛtti nimitta* of the word *gavaya*"? The forester understood the city dweller in this way. But he was not at the moment in a position to show ostensively what was a *gavaya* or to which the word *gavaya* applies. For right now, he is in the town and *gavaya* is in the forest. So he tells the city dweller what is the *upalakṣaṇa* of *gavaya*. The similarity to cow (*go-sādṛśya*) is *upalakṣaṇa*. This similarity is perceptible and is suggestive of *gavayatva*. We give an example. *Kambugrīvā* is suggestive of *ghaṭatva jāti*. Besides, similarity of *gavya* to cow consists in the common features like such *avayavas* as horn, tail, etc. These features are perceptually evident at the moment in the cow; for it is there before the city dweller. After he has been told about this *upalakṣaṇa*, later the city dweller goes to the forest. He there sees an animal, sees in it the similarity about which he heard before, and remembers the content of the statement of analogy. Now the city dweller with the help of *tarka* comes to know that *gavayatva viśiṣṭa dharmī gavaya śabda vācyaḥ*. This knowledge that the particular (animal) which has *gavayatva* is the referent of the word *gavaya* is a distinctive kind of knowledge, and it is the result of *upamāna* (cf. ibid.: 86-87). We shall return to this point again in the next section of this chapter.

IV

Gaṅgeśa has incidentally discussed some alternative views which he rejected also (cf. ibid.: 87-98). He concludes his discussion by offering a definition of analogy as means of knowledge called *upamiti*. In other words, he defines *upamāna* as the special means which is instrumental in bringing about *upamiti*; and *upamiti* is the knowledge that the thing which has the *pravr̥tti-nimitta* associated with the word in question is the referent of the word. *Lakṣaṇantu upamiti karaṇatvam* (ibid.: 98). Two points should be noted about this definition. In the first place, this definition is significantly different from the definition of Gautama. It is also different from the definition we find in Śabarasvāmī, Prabhākara, Kumārila, Śālikanātha and many others. The second point to note is that the definition is in terms of *upamiti*. If now *upamiti* is defined, in terms of *upamāna*, as the knowledge which results from *upamāna*, then there will be circularity. Gaṅgeśa is aware of this, so in the very next sentence he tells us that *upamiti* is not to be defined as knowledge caused by *upamāna*. It is to be defined as what has *upamititva jāti* or what has the universal character *upamititva*: *upamititvañca jātiḥ*. It seems that Gaṅgeśa would admit that this *jāti* has in support of it the evidence of the second order perception of cognitive state which has the form *upaminomi*. It follows that

> *upaminomi iti anuvyavasāya sākṣika jāti viśeṣa* (*upamititva*) *hi upamiti lakṣaṇaṁ*. – Gaṅgeśa 1990, III: 83

Pragalbhācārya has made reference to such *anuvyavasāya*. Gaṅgeśa himself has raised the question. Are we justified to admit a distinct class or universal called *upamititva* and regard *upamiti* as a distinct class of knowledge? Gaṅgeśa says in reply that where causes are different the effects must be of different kinds.

It may be noted that Gaṅgeśa does not define *upamāna* as knowledge of similarity. The idea seems to be that knowledge of similarity *qua* knowledge of similarity is not the *upamāna pramāṇa*. It is *upamāna pramāṇa* only as the *karaṇa* of *upamiti*. The point involved here is quite subtle. In the Nyāya tradition, *upamiti* is understood as that type of knowledge which has knowledge of similarity as its special means or cause:

> *upamitau sādṛśya jñānasya . . . karaṇatvāt.*
>
> – Viśvanātha 1377 (Baṅgābda): 122.
> See also verse 79, p. 191

But one does not necessarily come to have the knowledge of *śakti* (i.e. the meaning relation) whenever one has experience of similarity between any two things. Therefore the more accurate way of putting the two is the following. *Upamāna* is what is the special means of *upamiti*. *Upamāna* character of *upamāna* of a thing (knowledge) consists in its being the special means of *upamiti*. It does not consist in its being the knowledge of similarity. But as we know that *karaṇa* of *upamiti* is a knowledge. So what is the nature of this knowledge which is the *karaṇa* or *upamāna* in relation to *upamiti*? Gaṅgeśa suggests:

> *upamiti karaṇaṁ upamānam, tacca sādṛśya jñānam eva.*

But what is *upamiti*? Gaṅgeśa defines *upamiti* in terms of *upamititva jāti* (*upamititvañca jātiḥ* – Gaṅgeśa 1990, III: 98).

In *Bhāṣā Paricchedaḥ*, Viśvanātha has shown how each of the four types of knowledge or *pramā* may be defined in terms of the respective class character or universal (c.f. Viśvanātha 1377 (Baṅgābda): 264f). In his paper "Alternative Definitions of *Pratyakṣa*", Pradyot Kumar Mukhopadhyay (1981) made two points: (1) He showed with reference to Viśvanātha's definition of *pratyakṣa* (perception) in terms of class character, that such definition cannot work independently. If it is to work then there must be some independent means to identify certain instance of the thing (knowledge) to be defined. That is in order to understand or apply the definition of *pratyakṣa* in terms of *jāti* we must somehow identify first some instance of knowledge as *pratyakṣa*. The same must be true about the definition of *upamiti* suggested by Gaṅgeśa. The second point which Mukhopadhyay made in that article is the following. In answer to the question what could be Viśvanātha's source for the definition of different *pramā*s in terms of respective class character, he suggested that Gadādhara's commentary on Raghunātha's commentary on Gaṅgeśa's *Anumānacintāmaṇi* is the source. It seems he thought that Viśvanātha could not have developed and derived this technique of definition in terms of class character from Gaṅgeśa himself. It appears that he did not consult or consider Gaṅgeśa's *Upamānacintāmaṇi* at that time. For here Gaṅgeśa explicitly defined *upamiti* in terms of class character. I believe that Gaṅgeśa's definition of *upamiti* is the source from where Gadādhara or Viśvanātha or both of them derived the insight and the technique directly.

6

Faultless to a Fault?
An Epilogue to a Realist View

We may not ignore or uphold a concept or an entity or a person, whatever that may be, merely by our respective liking and disliking. *Upamāna* is such an epistemological concept in Indian philosophical literature as to require more sustained discussion. Most of the philosophers denied it but could not ignore the concept. The negative importance is immense. It may be that for this reason, the stalwart philosophers in the Nyāya tradition in different centuries took the responsibility for defending *upamāna pramāṇa* as an irreducible independent source of knowledge. In the early stage of systematic Nyāya philosophy, other than the Cārvākas, the strongest opposition came from the Buddhists. The debate continued till the eleventh century. In the meantime, other schools also raised objections. The objections started from questioning the definition of this source of knowledge, its independence, regarding the nature of the resulting knowledge and many other questions. In the literature we find the Nyāya answer. At least we can understand what will be the Nyāya standpoint against such objections. As this is the situation, titles of my both books are given sarcastically, Nyāya concept of *upamāna* is really dishonoured by most of the philosophers or truly speaking by all the philosophers other than those belonging to the Nyāya school. Even Bhāsarvajña, Nyāyaikadeśī has denied the independence of *upamāna*. The Mīmāṁsā school, though they have admitted it, took *upamāna* totally in a different sense. So it is also a kind of negative attitude. But this is honoured by the stalwart Nyāya philosophers,

Gautama, Udayanācārya and Gaṅgeśa. To Udayanācārya, an eleventh-century Nyāya philosopher, the Buddhist advanced the strongest opposition. So he tried to contend the Buddhist position. We find that he wrote two books only in relation to the notion of self – *Ātmatatva-viveka* and *Nyāyakusumāñjaliḥ* – beside other books. In the latter book, he writes:

> *sambandhasya paricchedaḥ saṁjñayāḥ saṁjñinā saha pratyakaṣdersādhyatvāupamāna phalam biduḥ.*
>
> — Udayanācārya, 1957, Karika 3.10

In English: word (name) meaning relation cannot be known by perception, etc. so *upamāna* is to be accepted. If we go to the Indian history, we see that after the eleventh century Buddhism was declining. As a result, non-Buddhist traditions became prominent. Philosophical dialogue streamlined to Nyāya and Mīmāṁsā mainly. Accordingly, Gaṅgeśa's strong opposition was directed toward the Mīmāṁsā school. Gaṅgeśa has shown the defect in Mīmāṁsā position and the positive feature of Nyāya theory of *upamāna*. He represents the faultless to a fault. But what is the nature of his perfection?

In my previous book all the inner objections were answered from the Nyāya position. The strong external objection I have placed in the present book and tried to give answer from the Nyāya texts. Here Gaṅgeśa's position comes to the forefront as he has tried to perfect the Nyāya defence. Take the issue of similarity (*sādṛśya*), for example. The issue has been treated differently by the Mīmāṁsakas and Gaṅgeśa. The two monographs that I have prepared are on epistemology but the discussion on similarity is metaphysical. I am compeled to bring this metaphysical discussion to combat the Mīmāṁsā position. In Indian philosophy, one of the most striking features is that all the different aspects of epistemology, metaphysics, ethics go together. A philosopher doing epistemology cannot ignore metaphysics. The discussion of similarity by Gaṅgeśa makes that point clear. Both Nyāya and Mīmāṁsā admit that this similarity is involved in the process of *upamāna* and according to the Mīmāṁsakas in the resulting knowledge as well.

Before I end I should clarify a few points. In which sense have I defended the Nyāya theory of *upamāna*? I have not unconditionally rejected the other positive theory of *upamāna*, viz. the Mīmāṁsā theory of *upamāna*. It is normally expected that I should make a comparative assessment of these two theories of *upamāna* and show that Nyāya theory of *upamāna* is better than the Mīmāṁsā theory of *upamāna*. But one of the major things which I have learned from my present work is that such a comparison is not possible here. The controversy about *upamāna* is importantly different from many other familiar philosophical disputes. Take the example of the controversy between the Mīmāṁsakas and the Naiyāyikas about the seat (*āśraya*) of *śakti*. The Mīmāṁsakas say that the universals like cowness alone are the seat of word-meaning (*pada śakti*). A part of the Nyāya position is that it is not true that the universals alone are the seat of *śakti*. Similarly, the Prābhākaras hold that *sādṛśya* is an independent category (of being). The Naiyāyikas categorically deny this. These are, therefore, some of the examples of straightforward controversies. The two groups of philosophers in these cases are directly opposed to each other, and their views are mutually exclusive. Accordingly both their views cannot be true.

When I began the present work, I used to hold the popular belief that the controversy about *upamāna* is of the same kind. But I soon realized that the controversy between the Naiyāyikas and the Mīmāṁsakas about *upamāna* is uniquely different. The Nyāya theory of *upamāna* and the Mīmāṁsā theory of *upamāna* are not two different and incompatible version of a single theory. For the Mīmāṁsā theory of *upamāna* is not a theory about how we learn word-meaning. Similarly the Nyāya theory of *upamāna* is not about how we know that an imperceptible thing resembles a perceptible thing. They are actually two different theories about two different things. The Nyāya theory of *upamāna* is a theory of how we learn the meaning of words in certain cases, e.g. *go–gavaya* case. The Mīmāṁsā theory of *upamāna* is a theory of how we know in certain cases, e.g. *go–gavaya* case, that the unperceived cow is similar to the perceived *gavaya*. How can we compare theories that are so different? There seems to be no common point. How can we make any comparative assessment?

Three questions will arise. First, can I clarify further the important difference between the Nyāya theory of *upamāna* and the Mīmāṁsā theory of *upamāna*? Second, if the two theories are so widely different, then why both are described in the same way as the theory of *upamāna*? Third, if comparative assessment of the two theories is not possible, how can we say that we have defended the Nyāya theory of *upamāna*? We shall answer the third question first. Then we shall discuss the first two questions together. I shall say in what sense I have defended the Nyāya theory of *upamāna*. I shall also say in which sense I have not defended the Nyāya theory of *upamāna*. We have defended the Nyāya theory of *upamāna* in the sense that we have answered the objections and criticisms which were brought against it. Among these criticisms some were made by the Mīmāṁsakas who advocate Mīmāṁsā theory of *upamāna*. So we can say that we have defended the Nyāya theory of *upamāna* against the Mīmāṁsakas also.

We do not say that we have defended the Nyāya theory of *upamāna* by rejecting or disproving the Mīmāṁsā theory of *upamāna*. But we have criticized and refuted many doctrines of the Mīmāṁsā theory of *upamāna*. So far we could even say that we have rejected the Mīmāṁsā theory of *upamāna*. But our point is that there is no necessary connection between rejecting the Mīmāṁsā theory of *upamāna* and defending the Nyāya theory of *upamāna*. For these two theories are not two opposite theories of the same thing. Therefore from the rejection of one it does not follow that the other is proved.

The Mīmāṁsakas advocate the Mīmāṁsā theory of *upamāna* and they also criticize the Nyāya theory of *upamāna*. But we want to say that the Mīmāṁsā criticisms of the Nyāya theory of *upamāna* and the Mīmāṁsā's adherence to the Mīmāṁsā theory of *upamāna* are not necessarily connected. So one may not accept the Mīmāṁsā theory of *upamāna* but may still accept the Mīmāṁsā criticisms against the Nyāya theory of *upamāna*. So we have kept the two separate. We do not even want to reject the Mīmāṁsā theory of *upamāna* altogether. It has also some good points. Even a Naiyāyika can accept the Mīmāṁsā theory of *upamāna* to have some value if he considers it as a theory of comparison. This is our explanation for saying that we have defended the Nyāya theory of *upamāna* in the sense that we have answered all the criticisms against it including the criticisms which the advocates of the Mīmāṁsā theory of *upamāna* brought up. But we do not want to claim that our defence of the Nyāya theory of *upamāna* entails or presupposes the rejection of the Mīmāṁsā theory of *upamāna*.

Now we may discuss the first and second questions. In course of doing research for this book pertaining to the nature of perfection in Gaṅgeśa's view on *upamāna*, I could gain much clarity. This so-called debate between the Nyāya theory of *upamāna* and the Mīmāṁsā theory of *upamāna* is uniquely different. The Nyāya theory of *upamāna* is a theory about how we learn word-meaning in cases like *go–gavaya*. According to the advocates of the Nyāya theory of *upamāna*, the source from which we derive knowledge of word-meaning in such cases is (a) an independent source of knowledge. They also think that (b) this source of knowledge should be called *upamāna*. The Mīmāṁsakas may not deny that sometimes similarity is used to teach word-meaning. They may also accept the Nyāya description of the process of knowledge of word-meaning by analogy. But they will deny (a). They say that if the knowledge of word-meaning by analogy is a process as described by the

Naiyāyikas, then it is not different from the process of knowing from words (*śabda pramāṇa*). What a Mīmāṁsaka will say about (b)? Can a Mīmāṁsaka say that the Naiyāyikas are right when they say the following? The source from which the knowledge of *śakti* is derived in *go–gavaya* case, according to the Nyāya theory of *upamāna*, is rightly called *upamāna*. Now in the *go–gavaya* case, *go* is the *upamāna* and *gavaya* is the *upameya*. We shall explain this presently. But we would like to say first that according to the Nyāya theory of *upamāna* the process of *śakti jñāna* involves the knowledge of *go* (*upamāna*). For the process involves a statement (*atideśa vākya*) which involves reference to *go*. Again the process involves a perception of similarity of *go* or the *upamāna*. So far the process of deriving the knowledge of *śakti* according to the Nyāya theory of *upamāna* may be called *upamāna pramāṇa*.

But here also there is doubt. The Naiyāyikas themselves have raised a question. Is statement or verbal knowledge of analogy (similarity) necessary for *upamāna*? In his commentary *Rahasya* on (*Śabda*) *Cintāmaṇi* of Gaṅgeśa, Mathuranatha, while dealing with the point why *śabda* is considered after *upamāna*, has discussed the point. One can say that *śabda* should be discussed before *upamāna* because in order to know word-meaning by analogy, there must first be *śabda pramāṇa*, namely, *atideśa vākya*. Mathuranatha here answers this objection and defends Gaṅgeśa (and generally Nyāya) way of ordering the *pramāṇa*s. He says that it is possible that in answer to the question "what like is *gavaya*?" (*kīdṛk gavaya*), nobody utters a statement of analogy. Instead, a picture of *gavaya* is shown to the inquirer. Here *upamiti* or *upamāna* (perception of similarity) is not preceded by *vākya* or *atideśa vākya* (Mathuranatha 1990, IV(I): 4).[1] If this defence of Mathurānātha is accepted, then there are cases where *atideśa vākya* is not employed. In such cases the knowledge of *śakti* is

---

[1] There is a long and interesting discussion on this point. See also Rucidatta 1991: 1.

not preceded by *atideśa vākya* or the knowledge of *atideśa vākya*. Here the process of *śakti jñāna* does not involve *upamāna*. So the process of *śakti jñāna* cannot rightly be described as *upamāna*. If *atideśa vākya* were a necessary part of knowing *śakti* in *go-gavaya* case, then we could say that the process is *upamāna*.

It seems on the other hand that the Mīmāṁsakas use the word *upamāna* first in the sense of the opposite of *upameya*. Second, they use the word *upamāna* as the act or knowledge of comparison. Both these senses are supported by dictionary. The Mīmāṁsā theory of *upamāna* is primarily a theory of comparison. It aims at explaining how we can know the *upamāna* in cases like *go–gavaya* or *āgneya–saurya*. In an act of comparison, the *upameya* is the thing which is compared. The *upamāna* is the thing with which some other thing is compared. Now a theory about the thing which is *upamāna*, may legitimately be called a theory of *upamāna*. Therefore the Mīmāṁsā sense of *upamāna pramāṇa* is quite legitimate. From this point of view *go* (in the *go–gavaya* case) is *upamāna*. And the Mīmāṁsā theory of *upamāna* seeks to explain how we can have knowledge of the *upamāna* in the *go–gavaya* case. For here *upamāna* cannot be known by perception. The knower in our example is in the forest at present and *upamāna*, the cow, is in the city. The conditions for inferential knowledge also do not hold. And the Mīmāṁsakas do not take *atideśa vākya* to be a necessary condition. Parthasarathi Mishra (1913: 208) does not even mention *atideśa vākya* in the statement of Mīmāṁsā view of *upamāna*. Only once he brings reference to *śabda* (not to *atideśa vākya*) but at once rejects it. He says *śabdatvam tu na śaṁkhyameva* (ibid.: 213). Ramkrishna Mishra refers to *atideśa vākya* but says that it is not a necessary factor. Thus according to the analysis *yena upamiyate tadupamāna*, *go*, in our example is *upamāna*. And the Mīmāṁsā theory is the knowledge of this *upamāna*. So it can be said to be the theory of *upamāna*.

But the cow or *go* is the *upamāna* only in relation to certain other thing which is *upameya* (here *gavaya*) and only in the context of comparison. Thus comparing or noting similarity (i.e. *sādṛśya jñāna*) is essentially involved in *upamāna–upameya* case or *go–gavaya* case. The Mīmāṁsā theory of *upamāna* also deals with the knowledge of *sādṛśya*. Using the language and technique of Navya-Nyāya, we may show the *ākāra* (form) of this knowledge of *upamāna*. It is *upamāna viśeṣyaka, upameyapratiyogikasādṛśya prakāraka jñāna*. Or the *ākāra* is *gavaya sādṛśī gauḥ*. Further this knowledge is caused by another knowledge. This knowledge has three features: (1) it is perceptual; (2) it has the *upameya* (*gavaya*) for its subject; and (3) it has *upamāna*, i.e. (*go*) *pratiyogika sādṛśya* as predicate.

A Naiyāyika may not reject the Mīmāṁsā theory of *upamāna* as described above. They may agree that sometimes we may have *upamāna viśeṣyaka jñānam* caused by *upameya viśeṣyaka jñānam*. But they themselves are interested not in the question how in cases like *go–gavaya*, we may know by *upamāna*. They are more interested in the question how knowledge of similarity with *upamāna* helps us in knowing the reference of the name of the *upameya padārtha*. From the philosophical point of view the semantic question "how the reference of a certain term is determined (in certain context)" is more important. It is not so important to ask how the imperceptible (at the moment) term of a comparison is known. But why is the theory which deals with the semantic question called a theory of *upamāna*? The reason is this. What distinguishes a pair of things as the pair which comprises *upamāna* and *upameya* is that the things resemble each other. Utilizing one's knowledge of similarity between a pair of resembling thing, one may teach word-meaning to another man. This another man is one who knows one of the things of the pair and its name (*go* – *go*); but he does not know what is the meaning of the name of the other thing in the pair.

But is it legitimate to call this process *upamāna*? In what sense can the Naiyāyika call it *upamāna*? In the classical literature, a few clear uses of the expression of *upamāna* are there. In the *sūtra* 1.1.6 Gautama said *prasiddha sādharmyāt sāddhya sādhanam upamānam*. Vātsyāyana in his commentary of *Nyāya-Sūtra* 1.1.1 says *upamānam upanaya*. Gautama has not spoken about *upamāna* in the *sūtra* 1.1.38. Anyway, these two uses of *upamāna* are not the same. *Upamāna* in the sense of *upanaya* comes closer to the sense in which *upamāna* is discussed in the Mīmāṁsā theory of *upamāna*. But characteristic sense in which *upamāna* is used in the Nyāya theory of *upamāna* is found in the Gautama *sūtra* 1.1.6. Now how these two senses can be reconciled? Phanibhusan Tarkavagisa has given answer to this question by taking que from what Vātsyāyana has said at the end of his commentary on *sūtra* 1.1.6.

But we think that we can justify the description of the Nyāya theory of knowledge of *śakti* in the *go–gavaya* case in this way. Here the resulting knowledge is the knowledge of the reference of the name of the *upameya padārtha*; it is the knowledge of *gavaya padavācyatva*. And this knowledge results from a perception and a memory. The perception has the following form. It is *upameya* (*gavaya*) *viśeṣyaka upamāna* (*go*) *pratiyogika-sādṛśya prakāraka jñānam*. This is the same as in the Mīmāṁsā theory of *upamāna*. For there also perception of *sādṛśya* is admitted. The form of the memory causing the *śakti jñāna* here is determined by the form of the *atideśa vākya*. For, this memory is the memory of the content of the *atideśa vākya*. This *atideśa vākya* again involves the names of both *upamāna* and *upameya*. Therefore *upamāna–upameya* and their knowledge are all through present in the Nyāya theory of *pada śakti jñāna* in the *go-gavaya* case. Hence some justification is there for describing this theory as the theory of *upamāna*.

I will briefly state one or two more points which came to light during this research. *Upamāna* is a theme which is being discussed in the Nyāya school from the time of Gautama. This theme is also being discussed in the Mīmāṁsā school from the time of Śabarasvāmī. It is a popular belief that Indian philosophy is generally repetitive. But we have noted that these theory had their history of development. Sometimes the development is very marked. At other times the development is slow, subtle and almost imperceptible. Let us look at one or two examples. Bhāsarvajña is a Naiyāyika. But he rejected *upamāna pramāṇa*. He claimed at the same time that he had not gone against the spirit of Nyāya or Gautama. Vyomaśivācārya is a Vaiśeṣika. But he accepted *śabda pramāṇa*. Gāgābhaṭṭa's account of *upamāna* clearly shows how in his hands the Mīmāṁsā theory of *upamāna* had developed under the influence of Navya-Nyāya. Vallabhācārya came after Udayanācārya. But he did not accept the authority of Udayanācārya. He did not join the syncretic school of Vaiśeṣika of which Udayanācārya was the founder. Lastly, Gaṅgeśa was a great admirer of Udayanācārya. Some great scholars have even said that Gaṅgeśa borrowed all the important things from the predecessors. But Gaṅgeśa criticized strongly the way Udayanācārya sought to defend the Vaiśeṣika scheme of seven categories. On the positive side he introduced a new definition of *upamāna*, and a new technique of defining things like *upamāna* in terms of their class characters. It was not known so long that Gaṅgeśa invented this technique of definition. Again we have discovered how difficult it is to defend the way in which Gautama or the Naiyāyikas have ordered the different *pramāṇa*s they admit. We have also found a novel way of defending the Nyāya scheme of *pramāṇa*s which involve a particular way of ordering a particular number of *pramāṇa*s.

I would like to conclude by making reference to the best contribution which has been made in recent times to the scholarship in the field of *upamāna* by one of the greatest Naiyāyikas of our time, Pandit Badrinath Shukla who passed away in the early 1990s. In 1986 he contributed a paper in Hindi with the title "Navya-Nyāya mein Upamāna Pramāṇa" in a seminar on Enterprise of Navya Nyāya, organized in NISTADS, New Delhi. In this paper Badrinathji listed the development of Nyāya theory of *upamāna* in the hands of the Navya-Naiyāyikas.

It has also been discussed that the difference of form of *upamiti* – *gavaya gavaya padavācya* and *ayam gavaya padavācya* – is so important.

Thus what Gaṅgeśa has done in his exposition on *upamāna* is very unique in the realist tradition of Indian philosophy. He has not only developed the most vigorous defence of Nyāya position vis-à-vis the Mīmāṁsā objection to it, he has also shown the method of reducing similarity to universal and thus giving place to the law of parsimony to make his view more logical. In this sense, Gaṅgeśa's contribution to Indian epistemology is really great. He is not only faultless, and more simple in his explanation on *upamāna* but by an extension of the argument represents logically a more realist stand in Indian philosophy.

Bibliography

[English alphabetical order of the first name in case of Indian authors, and second name in case of foreign authors has been followed.]

Annaṁbhaṭṭa or Annaṁbhaṭṭopādhyāya, 1976, *Tarkasaṁgrahaḥ* with *Dīpikā*, edited with his own translation and elucidation in English by Gopinath Bhattacharya, Calcutta: Progressive Publishers.

Aparārkadeva, 1961, *Nyāyamuktāvalī on Nyāyasāraḥ of Bhāsarvajña*. See Bhāsarvajña, 1961.

Badrinatha Shukla, "Navya-Nyāya mein Upamāna Pramāṇa" (unpublished paper) presented in the seminar "Enterprise of Navya Nyāya: A Tradition of Medieval and Modern Indian Logic", NISTADS, New Delhi, 1986.

Bhāsarvajña, 1961, *Nyāyasāraḥ*, ed. Subrahmanya Śāstrī with the commentaries of *Nyāyamuktāvalī* by Aparākadeva and *Nyāyakalānidhi* by Ānandānubhavācārya, Madras.

———, 1968, *Nyāyasāraḥ*, with the author's own commentary *Nyāyabhūṣaṇam*, ed. Swami Yogindrananda, Varanasi: Chowkhamba Vidyabhavan.

Bhimacarya Jhalkikar, 1978, *Nyāyakośaḥ*, Poona: The Bhandarkar Oriental Research Institute.

Bhūtanātha Saptatīrtha, *Mīmāṁsā Darśanaṁ* (in Bengali), part I, Calcutta: Basumati Sahitya Mandir, 1345 Baṅgābda.

Bimal Krishna Matilal, 1986, *Perception: An Essay on Classical Indian Theories of Knowledge*, Oxford: Clarendon Press.

Dharmakīrti, 1953, *Pramāṇavārttikam*, ed. Rāhul Sāṅkṛtyāyana with Prajñākaragupta's *Pramāṇavārttikabhāṣyam* or *Vārttikālaṁkāraḥ*, Patna: Kasi Prasad Jayaswal Research Institute.

———, 1955, *Nyāyabindu*, ed. with Dharmottara's Commentary *Nyāyabindu Ṭīkā* and Durveka's sub-commentary *Dharmottarapradīpa* by Pandit Dalsukhbhai Malvania, Patna: Kasi Prasad Jayaswal Research Institute.

———, 1968, *Pramāṇavārttikam*, ed. Svami Dvarikadas Shastri with the commentary *Vṛtti* of Manorath Nandin, Varanasi: Bauddha Bharati.

Dharmottara, 1955, *Nyāyabindu Ṭīkā* in Dharmakīrti.

Gāgābhaṭṭa, 1933, *Bhāṭṭacintāmaṇi* (*Tarakapādaḥ*), ed. Pandit Surya Naṛayan Sukla, Banaras: Chowkhamba Sanskrit Series Office.

Gaṅgeśopādhyāya or Gaṅgeśa, 1970, *Anumānacintāmaṇi*, ed. with *Dīdhiti* and *Gādādharī* by Vindhesvari Prasad Dvivedi and others (two volumes), Varanasi: Chowkhamba.

———, 1983, *Tattvacintāmaṇi* (Upamānakhaṇḍa) with the commentary *Raśmicakra* by Gokulnatha Upadhyaya, ed. Pandit Ramsevak Jha, Darbhanga: Kamesvarsimha Darbhanga Sanskrit Visvavidyalaya.

———, 1983, *Tattvacintāmaṇi* (Upamānakhaṇḍa) with the commentary *Prāgalbhī* by Pragalbhācārya, edited by Gourinatha Shastri, Varanasi: Sampurnananda Sanskrit Visvavidyalaya.

———, 1990, *Tattvacintāmaṇi* (vols. I-IV), ed. Kamakhyanatha Tarkavagisa, with the commentaries *Māthurī*, *Kṛṣṇakāntī* (*Dīpanī*), etc., Calcutta: Chowkhamba Sanskrit Pratisthan, repr.

Gautama, 1985, *Nyāyadarśanam*, with *Bhāṣya*, *Vārttika*, *Tātparyaṭīkā* and *Vṛtti*, ed. Taranath Tarkatirtha, New Delhi: Munshiram Manoharlal.

———, 1967, *Nyāyadarśanam*, ed. Anantalal Thakur with *Bhāṣya*, *Vārttika*, *Tātparyaṭīkā* and *Pariśuddhi*, Darbhanga: Mithila Institute.

Gokulnatha Upadhyaya, 1983, *Raśmicakra Vyākhyā*, A commentary on *Tattvacintāmaṇi of Gaṅgeśa* (Upamānakhaṇḍa). See Gaṅgeśa.

Gopinath Bhattacharya, 1976, *Translation and Elucidation of Tarkasaṁgraha*. See Annaṁbhaṭṭa.

Gopinath Kaviraj, 1982, *The History and Bibliography of Nyāya-Vaiśeṣika Literature*, Varanasi: Sampurnananda Sanskrit University.

Guṇaratna, 1986, *Tarkarahasya Dīpikā* (a commentary on *Ṣaḍdarśana Samuccaya* by Haribhadra), ed. L. Suali, Calcutta: The Asiatic Society, Reprint.

Haridasa Bhattacharya, 1962, *Vivṛtti* (*Vyākhyā*) in Sanskrit on *Nyāyakusumāñjaliḥ* (*Kārikā*) by Udayanācārya, ed. with Hindi elucidation by Pandit Vishveshvar Siddhanta Siromani, Chowkhamba.

Harrison, Bernard, 1979, *An Introduction to the Philosophy of Language*, London: Macmillan.

Jagadīśa Tarkālaṁkāra, 1930, *Sūkti* (a commentary on *Praśastapāda-Bhāṣya*), See Praśastapāda.

———, 1973, *Śabdaśakti Prakāśikā* with *Kṛṣṇakānti* and *Prabodhinī*, ed. Pandit Dhundhiraj Shastri, Varanasi: The Chowkhamba Sanskrit Series Office.

Jaimini, 1883, *Mīmāṁsāsūtra*, ed. with *Śābarabhāṣya* by Jīvānanda Vidyāsāgara, Calcutta.

———, 1934, *Mīmāṁsāsūtra*. See Bhūtanātha.

Jayantabhaṭṭa, 1936, *Nyāyamañjarī*, ed. Pandit Surya Narayan Shukla, Varanasi: Chowkhamba Sanskrit Series Office (Reprint 1971).

Jayapuri Narayan Bhatta, 1961, *Nyāyasiddhi* on *Prakaraṇapañcikā* in Śālikanātha.

Jñānaśrīmitra, 1959, *Jñānaśrīmitranibandhāvalī*, ed. Prof. Anantalal Thakur, Patna: Kasi Prasad Jayaswal Research Institute.

Kamalākarbhaṭṭa, 1987, *Mīmāṁsākutūhalam*, ed. with notes by Pattabhiram Shastri, Varanasi: Sampurnananda Sanskrit University.

Krishnakanta Vidyavagisha, 1990, *Dīpanī*. See Gaṅgeśa, 1990.

Kumārila Bhaṭṭa, 1978, *Ślokavārttikam* with *Nyāyaratnākara* by Parthasarathi Mishra, ed. Svami Dvarikadas Shastri, Varanasi: Tara Publications.

Madhusudan Nyayacharya (ed.), 1980, *Translation and Exposition of Śabdaśaktiprakāśikā by Jagadīśa Tarkālaṁkāra*, vol. I, Calcutta: Sanskrit College.

Manikaṇa, 1960, *A Navya-Nyāya Manual*, ed. E.R. Sreekrishna Sarma, Madras: The Adyar Library and Research Centre.

Mathuranatha Tarkavagisa, 1990, *Rahasya* (*ṭīkā*) on *Tattvacintāmaṇi*, in Gaṅgeśa.

Nārāyaṇa Bhaṭṭa, 1975, *Mānameyodaya*, ed. with English translation by C. Kunhan Raja and S.S. Suryanarayan Shastri, second edn., Madras: The Adyar Library.

Pañcānan Śāstrī, *Muktāvalīsaṁgraha* in Viśvanātha Nyāya Pañcānan, 1377 Baṅgābda.

———, Translation and Elucidation in Bengali of *Tarkasaṁgraha* by Annaṁbhaṭṭopādhyāya, Nababharat Publishers, 1393 Baṅgābda.

Parthasarathi Mishra, 1913, *Śāstradīpikā*, with Ramkrishna's commentary *Yuktisneha-Prapūraṇī* and also with *Mayūkha Mālikā ṭīkā*, ed. Pandit Lakshman Shastri Dravida, Varanasi: Chowkhamba Sanskrit Series.

———, 1978, *Nyātaratnākara*, a commentary on *Ślokavārttika* of Kumārila. See Kumārila.

Phanibhusan Tarkavagisa, 1978, *Nyāya Paricaya* (in Bengali), Calcutta: West Bengal Book Board.

———, 1981-1989, *Nyāyadarśana*, 5 vols. containing translation and elucidation in Bengali of Nyāyasūtra and Vātsyāyanabhāṣya, Calcutta: West Bengal Book Board.

Potter, Karl H., 1974, *Encyclopedia of Indian Philosophies*, vol. I, New Delhi: Motilal Banarsidass.

Prabha Chandra, 1941, *Prameya Kamala Mārtaṇḍa*, ed. Mahendra Kumar Shastri, Bombay: Nirnaya Sagar Press, 2nd edn.

Prabhākara Miśra, 1934 *Bṛhatī* in Śabarasvāmī, 1934.

Pradyot Kumar Mukhopadhyay, 1981, "Alternative Definitions of Pratyakṣa", in K.K. Banerjee (ed.) *Mind, Language and Necessity*, Delhi: Macmillan.

———, 1984, *Indian Realism: A Rigorous Descriptive Metaphysics*, Calcutta: K.P. Bagchi and Company.

———, 1991, *The Nyāya Theory of Linguistic Performance* (*A New*

Interpretation of Tattvacintāmaṇi), Calcutta: K.P. Bagchi and Company.

Pragalbhācārya, 1983, *Prāgalbhī*, a commentary on *Tattvacintāmaṇi* of Gaṅgeśa (Upamānakhaṇḍa). See Gaṅgeśa.

Praśastapāda (Praśastadeva), 1930, *Praśastapādabhāṣyam*, ed. with *Sūkti-Setu* and *Vyomavatī* by Gopinath Kaviraj and Dhundiraj Shastri, Banaras: Chowkhamba Sanskrit Series.

———, 1963, *Padārthadharmasaṁgrahaḥ* (*Praśastapāda Bhāṣya*), ed. with *Nyāyakandalī* and Hindi translation by Durgadhar Jha, Varanasi: Varanaseya Sanskrita Visvavidyalaya.

Quine, Willard van Orman, 1960, *Word and Object*, Cambridge, MA: Massachusetts Institute of Technology.

———, 1977, "Natural Kinds", in Stephen P. Schwartz (ed.) *Meaning, Necessity and Natural Kinds*, Ithaca: Corwell University Press.

Raghunatha Siromani, 1968, *Avacchedakatva Niryukti*, ed. with his own commentary by Dattareya Shastri, Varanasi.

———, 1970, *Dīdhiti*, a commentary on Gaṅgeśa's *Anumānacintāmaṇi* in Gaṅgeśa.

Ramkrishna Mishra, 1913, *Yuktisneha-Prapūraṇī* in Parthasarathi, 1913.

Rāmānujācārya, 1956, *Tantrarahasya*, ed. Shama Shastri and K.S. Ramaswami Shastri with English Introduction, Baroda Oriental Institute.

Ramaswami Shastri, 1943, ed. with own Introduction, *Kāśikā* by Sucharita Mishra. See Sucharita.

Ratnakīrti, 1957, *Ratnakīrtinibandhāvalī*, Tibetan Sanskrit Works Series, vol. III, ed. Anantalal Thakur, Patna: Jayaswal Research Institute.

Rucidatta, 1991, *Prakāśa* (on *Śabdacintāmaṇi* by Gaṅgeśa), Calcutta: K.P. Bagchi and Company.

Śabarasvāmī, 1934, *Bhāṣya* on *Jaiminisūtra* ed. with Prabhākara Miśra's *Bṛhatī* and Śālikanātha Miśra's *Ṛjuvimalā Pañcikā*, by S.K. Ramanatha Shastri, University of Madras.

———, 1883, *Mīmāṁsā Bhāṣya*, ed. and published by Jivananda Vidyasagar Bhattacharya, Calcutta.

Śālikanātha Miśra, 1934, *Ṛjuvimalā Pañcikā* in Śabarasvāmī, 1934.

———, 1961, *Prakaraṇapañcikā* with *Nyāyasiddhi*, by Jaypuri Narayan Bhatta, ed. A. Subrahmanya Shastri, Varanasi: Banaras Hindu University.

Salmon, N.U., 1982, *Reference and Essences*, Oxford: Basil Blackwell.

Śaṅkara Miśra, 1934, *Kaṇṭhābharaṇam* on *Nyāyalīlāvatī* by Vallabhācārya, Varanasi: Chowkhamba Sanskrit Series.

———, 1930, *Upaskāra*, in Praśastapāda (to this edition, the copy of *Upaskāra*, I consulted was appended).

Śāntarakṣita, 1968, *Tattvasaṁgrahaḥ*, ed. with the commentary, *Pañjikā* of Kamalaśīla by Swami Dwarikadas Shastri, Varanasi: Bauddha Bharati.

Satischandra Vidyabhushan, 1978, *A History of Indian Logic*, Delhi: Motilal Banarsidass, repr.

Schwartz, Stephen P. (ed.), 1977, *Meaning, Necessity and Natural Kinds*, Ithaca: Corwell University Press.

Shiv Kumar, 1980, *Upamāna in Indian Philosophy*, Delhi: Eastern Book Linkers.

Siderits, Mark, 1991, *Indian Philosophy of Language*, Dordrecht, Boston: Kluwer Academic Publishers.

Subrahmanya Shastri, 1961, Introduction to *Prakaraṇa Pañcikā* of Śālikanātha. See Śālikanātha.

Sucharita Mishra, 1943, *Kāśikā*, a commentary on *Ślokavārttika* of Kumārila, ed. B.A. Ramaswami Shastri, Trivandrum: Anantasayan Visvavidyalaya.

Svarupa Pal, *Nyāyamate upamāna pramāṇa* (in Bengali), an unpublished Ph.D. dissertation of Jadavpur University, Supervisor, 1996.

Tachikawa, Musahi, 1981, *The Structure of the World in Udayana's Realism: A Study of Lakṣaṇāvalī and Kiraṇāvalī*, Dordrecht: Reidel Publishing Company.

Udayanācārya, 1941, *Nyāyakusumāñjaliḥ* (*Kārikā* and *Vṛtti*), ed. with his own commentary *Vistāra* by T. Vīrarāghavācārya Śiromaṇi, Tiruvadi.

———, 1957, *Nyāyakusumāñjaliḥ*, ed. with two commentaries by Dharmadatta Jha, Varanasi: Chowkhamba Sanskrit Series Office.

———, 1962, *Nyāyakusumāñjaliḥ* (*Kārikā*), ed. with Haridasa Bhattacharya's Sanskrit commentaries and his own Hindi commentary by Vishveshvar Siddhanta Shiromani, Varanasi: Chowkhamba Vidya Bhavan.

———, 1967, *Pariśuddhi* in Gautama.

Uddyotakara, *Vārttika* on *Vātsyāyana Bhāṣya* in Gautama 1967 and 1985.

Uma Chattopadhyay, 2009, *Dishonoured by Philosophers: Upamāna in Indian Epistemology*, New Delhi: D.K. Printworld.

Vācaspati Miśra, 1982, *Sāṁkhyatattvakaumudī* with the commentary *Adhyāpanā* by Narayana Chandra Goswami, Calcutta.

———, 1985, *Tātparyaṭīkā* on *Nyāya-Vārttika* of Uddyotakara. See Gautama.

Vallabhācārya, 1934, *Nyāyalīlāvatī*, ed. with the commentaries of Vardhamānopādhyāy, Śaṅkara Miśra and Bhagīratha Ṭhākkura (and with his own notes, etc. by Harihara Shastri) by Dhundiraja Shastri, Banaras: Chowkhamba.

Vardachari, V., 1987, "Nyāya-Vaiśeṣika Tradition", in *Philosophical Essays: Prof. Anantalal Thakur Felicitation Volume*, ed. Ramaranjan Mukhopadhyay, Calcutta: Sanskrit Pustak Bhandar.

Vardhamānopādhyāya, 1957, *Prakāśa*, a commentary on Udayana's *Savṛtti Nyāyakusumāñjaliḥ*. See Udayana.

Vātsyāyana, *Bhāṣya* on *Nyāyasūtra*. See Gautama, 1967, 1985.

Vindheswari Prasad Dvivedin (ed.), 1971, *Praśastapāda Bhāṣya Ṭīkā Saṁgraha* (This collection of commentaries of *Praśastapāda Bhāṣya* includes *Kaṇāda Rahasya* and *Tarkālaṁkāra Bhāṣya Parīkṣā*), Banaras: Chowkhamba Sanskrit Series.

Vīrarāghavācārya, T., 1941, *Kusumāñjaliḥ Vistāra*. See Udayana.

Viśvanātha, 1985, *Vṛtti* on *Nyāyasūtra*. See Gautama.

Viśvanātha Pañcānan, 1377 (Bhādra, Baṅgābda), *Bhāṣā-paricchedaḥ*, edited by Srimat Panchanan Bhattacharya (in Bengali), Calcutta: Sanskrit Pustak Bhandar.

———, 1989, *Nyāyasidhānta-Muktāvalī*, ed. Hariram Shukla Shastri, Varanasi: Chowkhamba Sanskrit Sansthan.

Vyomaśivācārya, 1930, *Vyomavatī* in Praśastapāda.

Index